NOTES FROM
A SWING STATE

Writing from Wales and America

Zoë Brigley (also Zoë Brigley Thompson), originally from Wales, is now assistant professor at the Ohio State University. She has three poetry collections *The Secret* (2007) and *Conquest* (2012), and her most recent, *Hand and Skull* (2019). She also co-edited the volume *Feminism, Literature and Rape Narratives* (2010). She is currently editing the *Bloomsbury Guide to Poetry in the UK and Ireland*.

NOTES FROM A SWING STATE

Writing from Wales and America

Zoë Brigley

PARTHIAN

Parthian, Cardigan SA43 1ED
www.parthianbooks.com
First published in 2019
© Zoë Brigley 2019
ISBN 978-1-912681-29-7
Editor: Susie Wild
Cover image 'Floral, Fluff, Flow' by Zena Blackwell
Cover design by www.theundercard.co.uk
Typeset by Elaine Sharples
Printed and bound by 4edge Limited, UK
Published with the financial support of the Welsh Books Council
British Library Cataloguing in Publication Data
A cataloguing record for this book is available from the British Library.

Oh yes, I'm broken but my limp
is the best part of me. And the way I hurt.
Gwyneth Lewis

— Source

CONTENTS

I. Girlhood, Motherhood, and

Arches

In the west of Utah, there stands a natural arch of entrada sandstone. Locally, it is known as the 'Schoolmarm's Bloomers' or the 'Chaps', but most people know it as the Delicate Arch. At one time, it was a sandstone fin. But gradually, the middle eroded, opened like a mouth to the long red desert and mountains beyond.

The first time I visited the Delicate Arch, I was driving cross-country with my husband Dan. We had been married just over a year, and in that time, I had miscarried two babies. I had given up trying to have children and suggested the drive to San Diego as a distraction for us both.

I was pregnant when I first went to live in the States, but a few days after I arrived in the US, we found out about the miscarriage. We had been called in to the obstetrician's office for my second ultrasound. Later, in a poem, I described what I saw on the screen as a 'tiny moon'. It wasn't moving, simply floating: slowly circuiting the fist of the womb.

Dan turned to the screen eagerly. He still didn't know. He hadn't been able to come to the first ultrasound screening back in Britain. He had never seen the baby alive – the quivering that signals life. Nothing was moving on the nurse's face.

Afterwards, I blamed the physician's assistant who had called us in for an ultrasound without checking the baby's heartbeat. We would never have been there, would never have seen the foetus dead on the monitor, if we'd had a more experienced doctor. She looked at us awkwardly afterwards, made us stand foolishly in the hall while she looked up some pamphlets on miscarriage.

3

We didn't realise it then, but this wouldn't be the last time that we lost a baby. After another failed pregnancy in the spring, I couldn't bear the thought of spending the long, hot summer in the small Pennsylvania town where we lived. So we started out to drive across America.

We had driven through the Midwest, lolloping hills in Kansas, the dreary flatness of the plains, and the Rockies rearing up from the even land like stern faces. By the time we reached Utah the land was changing again: red sandstone, ravines, boulders, pillars, fins, and cliffs. By the side of the road, a sign that read NO SOLICITING was pocked by bullet holes. Like most visitors, we stayed in the town of Moab. There was a motel called the Red Rock Lodge decorated in 1970s brown and cream. The view from the window showed nothing but hot, red rock. 'Like being on Mars', Dan said as we crawled into bed.

Moab – source

The next morning, we woke up at 5am and it was still dark. We drove into Arches National Park up the long, steep, winding road. You come to a plateau at the top and then the whole place opens out to a long, wide valley framed by sculptural shapes like long-bodied sentries.

Near the car park is the old log cabin that belonged to the family of a Civil War veteran named Wolfe. He came from Ohio in the nineteenth century, lived out in the emptiness for a good number of years and then returned to where he had come from. After the miscarriages, I began to wonder whether I too should admit defeat and catch the next plane back to Britain. Sometimes, I even imagined that the land itself had a hostile aspect, deadly with its winter snows, tornados, and devastating storms.

Arches was different though. Not a hostile land exactly, but rocks that had persisted for aeons, and were quite indifferent to human suffering. Crossing the bridge over the Salt Wash, a huge crow swooped down and landed on the handrail of the bridge, not so much threatening as curious. It held its ground as we passed by.

There was no one around when we started hiking. We

4

clambered up the steep, tilted slab of sandstone, the sunrise radiating the Salt Valley. It took a good thirty or forty minutes to scramble up and we still couldn't see the arch. At last we came upon a ledge with a sheer drop alongside, like a final challenge.

Writing in his 1968 memoir *Desert Solitaire*, Edward Abbey sums up the Delicate Arch, and the power it has over those who behold it. He writes: 'If Delicate Arch has any significance it lies, I will venture, in the power of the odd and unexpected to startle the senses and surprise the mind out of its ruts of habit, to compel us into a re-awakened awareness of the wonderful – that which is full of wonder'.

Seeing the arch so suddenly was wonder-full. But I asked myself, what is it about unexpected empty space that is so beautiful? Perhaps it signifies openness – a space that invites another in with generosity and selflessness. Or maybe it's just that emptiness conjures the spaces that most need filling in our own lives. Those things that we most desire and cannot have. The people we have lost. Failures that we lie awake at night regretting. Perhaps above all, it is lack made beautiful.

Then there's the fact too that the Delicate Arch will one day collapse. Like a beleaguered elder, it stands against the elements, but nothing lasts forever. Thinking these thoughts on the day of my visit, the O of the arch began to look like a cry of pain, and the legs braced against the wind seemed stoically determined. But there is always the need to humanise the land, to invoke a life or personality that never existed. I thought at last that there was nothing but stony silence and indifference in the red rock arch.

It's hard to explain exactly why, but sitting by the Delicate Arch that morning, I finally felt relief, as though a huge grief had been lifted. When we drove back into Moab later, we remembered that it was the 4th July, American Independence Day. People were putting up flags, or red, white, and blue decorations. Back at the motel, we threw together our belongings and drove back into the emptiness of Utah desert. Out there, beyond the narrow problems

5

of a few lives, we let the vastness of the red rocks fill us. As if a voice was saying that loss is inevitable, that it has existed since the desert came into being, and will go on existing long after the Delicate Arch is gone.

The Origin of the World

I start to like my father again when we are standing together looking at a painting. To begin, you would have to explain the place. The Musée D'Orsay in Paris was a railway station until 1939, and the great clock-faces on the exterior signal an obsession with timekeeping and travel. This particular painting is relatively small, and its intimacy is out of place under the arching glass roof covering the space where trains once ran. The museum is a public space and still has the feeling of a railway station with people hurrying to their next destination. In the middle of all this is a painting of a woman's genitals, and my father and I are standing together in front of it.

I have just turned eighteen, and my father has brought me to Paris as a birthday present. Some years before, my father moved with his new wife to the central lowlands of Scotland, but now he often rings on the phone. 'Just hop on a plane and come for a visit,' he says, but of course it is never that simple.

What my father does not know in Paris is that I am in a precarious place. A few years before, I swore that I would never have sex again: my first experiences were that awful. Not long after that, I slept with my best friend just for the sake of it, to get it over with.

I look at my father curiously. My experience of men is not huge. I can't trust that he will always be kind. Though he often laughs and jokes, something is not right with my father. When I ask my grandmother about him, she recalls one of his teachers stopping her outside the school gates and asking, 'What's wrong with your son?' She replied, 'I was hoping that you could tell me.'

He describes himself as the 'man who never was.' He is talking about the myriad jobs in which he never seemed to find satisfaction. He is talking about the journeys and trips he made – South America, Asia, Europe – never finding fulfilment. He is talking about the many women he took up with and later rejected.

I never heard my father tell anyone that he loved them, but he might have said so, in private, to one of the women he dated, or perhaps to my mother. Because he must have felt something. Much later, over dinner in Philadelphia, when I am a 'grown-up', my father will tell me that he never wanted to be a father, but a friend. I will say: 'I have enough friends.'

Still, the Paris galleries are enchanting, and I love looking at paintings with him. There is always some detail that he notices – a glint of light, a hint of a colour, a clue. We spend a long afternoon in the Musée D'Orsay, but one painting in particular strikes me: Courbet's 1866 work *The Origin of the World*.

At eighteen, I have not seen many pictures up-close of female genitalia. Once entering a sex shop for a dare, I glimpsed the vagina of pornography: the lurid gash of sex magazines. The painting is different: a gorgeous female torso, the breasts and head mainly covered by a sheet, a round stomach, the pubic hair and genitals, and thighs lounging open. I notice how visitors skirt around the picture as if nervous to be caught standing in front of it.

I stand by the painting with my father. He is never the type to be easily embarrassed by sexuality, and now he looks admiringly at the painting with genuine interest. He doesn't recoil from it in horror, or find it embarrassing, or think it is offensive. I find so much to like in him then: that he is never prudish about sex, but enjoys his relationships with women.

My father and I don't know each other very well, but in that moment in front of a painting in Paris, he helps me in some small way, because he celebrates the female body, and refuses shame. What is still to come is finding my own pleasure, and, eventually, I do.

Frankenstein and Reproductive Rights 200 Years On

This is a transcript of a talk given at the Ohio State University English department event, 'Frankenreads: Celebrating 200 Years of Mary Shelley's Frankenstein.' *The talk was given on 2ⁿᵈ November 2019 at the roundtable, 'The Power of* Frankenstein: *A Kaleidoscopic Roundtable.'*

'If we could perceive death as a part of pregnancy, we might just take women more seriously.' These words are taken from a 2018 article on 'Mothers as Makers of Death', published by Claudia Dey in the *Paris Review*, in which she affirms a darker alternative to what she describes as the Hallmark version of motherhood. Nineteenth-century author Mary Shelley, daughter of feminist trailblazer Mary Wollstonecraft, also understood that birth, reproduction, and death are not separate, but bound up intimately and inextricably. I want to revisit *Frankenstein* through the lens of reproduction, birth, and the maternal body. This seems a useful exercise, because at the heart of the famous book is Dr. Frankenstein's fatal dalliance with reproductive power, an example that might serve as a warning relevant to modern debates about reproductive rights, and taboos concerning maternal bodies.

Fiona Sampson's 2018 biography *In Search of Mary Shelley* takes great pains to portray experiences of birth and death, beginning with a graphic description of Mary Wollstonecraft giving birth to Shelley. The inept surgeon pulls away 'the afterbirth in pieces' with 'unsterile hands' without anaesthetic, an excruciating process that

Empty spaces in The unspeakable maternal.

condemned Wollstonecraft to die from septicaemia, suckling puppies instead of baby Mary who was taken away to protect her from the infection. It is still shocking to say this out loud, because there are still powerful taboos about maternal bodies, blood, afterbirth, placenta, the severed umbilical – not images for a Hallmark card. Wollstonecraft's story was so unspeakable that William Godwin, Shelley's father, marked the day of his wife's horrible death in his diary by ruling out the space.

Best essay on Utah

After eloping with Percy Bysshe Shelley to Europe, Mary Shelley's first child, Clara, was born premature, and died. She gave birth two more times before *Frankenstein* was published. Two more children died: William, and the second Clara died in Italy, though Shelley was soon pregnant again with Percy, the only one to survive to adulthood, and her final pregnancy ended in miscarriage. 'I was a mother,' Shelley wrote, 'and am no longer.' Frankenstein's monster resembles at times an animated version of that dynamic: death in life, or life in death.

It is no surprise then that Shelley's novel *Frankenstein* is preoccupied with this dynamic. More subtle and more powerful than its many film versions, *Frankenstein* is told through letters from sea captain, Robert Walton, who is on an expedition to the North Pole. Writing home to his sister, Walton tells how out on the ice, he spies a great figure driving a dog sled, and then in pursuit the emaciated traveller, Dr. Victor Frankenstein. Taken onboard ship, Frankenstein gradually tells his story: how in his youth he experimented with the power of creating life. Propelled by his mother's death, Frankenstein creates the famous monster of cultural mythology, but spurned by his maker and society, the monster tells his own tale of rejection with eloquence and power. The monster is so hideous that he is spurned and rejected by human beings. The revenge wreaked by the monster on Frankenstein brings about the deaths of his entire family, including his bride Elizabeth, which propels his pursuit of the monster into the Arctic.

In *Frankenstein,* the monster's birth is far less traumatic than Wollstonecraft's birthing of Shelley, though it occurs late at night like the result of a prolonged labour. The process beforehand is an ordeal for Dr. Frankenstein, who, like a woman about to give birth, secludes himself in his 'workshop of filthy creation.' The doctor's agony is guilt, when he sees 'the dull yellow eye of the creature open.' The monster springs to life painfully with a 'convulsive movement' recalling the fits of pain experienced by Wollstonecraft before her death. There is no welcome however, and the doctor will never love his creation as an effusive parent should. Instead Dr. Frankenstein describes the unspeakable ugliness of the newborn monster, but leaving much to the imagination, allowing us to conjure our own hideous vision, and very often in the novel, horror is expressed by silence.

The monster's ugliness though is definitely bound up with its make-up from pieces of different corpses stitched together, and the conjoining of bodies is very relevant to motherhood. In political wars over abortion in the United States, the state of Alabama's debate on a draconian anti-abortion bill revealed an interesting truth about the anti-abortion lobby and their view of mothers. When questioned about the difference between abortion and eggs destroyed in the process of in vitro fertilisation (IVF), republican representative Clyde Chambliss stated that the rules did not apply to an egg unless it was inside a woman, a statement that revealed deep mistrust of mothers as a whole. Mothers are posed here are a wild, chaotic force to be disciplined, while there is also anxiety about the idea of co-existing, of being part of the mother's body as an embryo. The mother's body is something to be feared and controlled rather than cherished.

This horror of the maternal body recalls a well-known story about Mary Shelley and her poet husband Percy Shelley during their infamous stay with Lord Byron at Villa Diodati. After Byron read a passage describing the putrescent, hideous breast of Duessa in Spenser's 'Christabel', Percy Shelley reportedly had a fit of anxiety, claiming that his wife reminded him of a woman who had eyes instead of nipples. Shelley had only just left off breastfeeding William, and the connection of the monstrous with his post-partum wife is extremely suggestive. In Frankenstein, the doctor wants to remove the child-bearing body from reproduction: 'so astonishing a power placed within my hands,' as when in Greek myth, Athena leaps fully formed from Zeus's head.

Birth, however, cannot be separated from the physical body. Dr. Frankenstein's creation is unspeakable, hideous, a product of the 'dissecting room' and 'slaughterhouse', yet the monster has a plan for a future in the supposedly uncivilised New World, and he is desirous of a mate so that he too can reproduce. Denied of that right, the monster murders the supportive cast of Dr. Frankenstein's family, including a child, and the women with whom the doctor might have created a family of his own. 'How dare you sport thus with life?' the monster cries, and we are not unsympathetic to his revenge. Like the anti-abortion legislators and lobbyists of the US or Northern Ireland, Dr. Frankenstein reveals not only his ugly sense of entitlement, but also the keenness of his fear in relation to the child-bearing body.

But to return to the night of the monster's birth, it is no coincidence that Frankenstein dreams of his dead mother, not as in life but here a corpse, representing the shadow side of Hallmark maternity. The doctor is horrified to see her maggot-infested body: a body that gave life once, gives it again in a horrific yet telling vision. Ultimately, the monster and the infested mother both represent fears about mortality and control which drive Frankenstein to produce life in the first place, the same fear in fact that drives modern day draconian rules around abortion and reproductive rights. The monster's eloquence, however, might allow the shadow side of maternity to speak once and for all.

Motherhood *is* Valuable
for the Creative Life

Whatever way you look at it, motherhood entails sacrifice. While the all-sacrificing mother is a reductive and unhelpful stereotype, it is a fact that as a mother you have to give up time, space, and energy for your children. This could mean stopping what you are doing every few hours to breastfeed. It could mean being interrupted by a steaming nappy. Or it could be the funnelling of creative energy into fort-building, cookie baking, imagining games, and planning adventures. Having two young children, I know all about this.

In her long poem about domesticity and womanhood, 'Letter from a Far Country', Gillian Clarke imagines male critics as seagulls that disturb domestic tranquillity with their shrieks. Where – they call – are your great works? And their cries are 'as cruel as greedy babies'. Clarke questions the compatibility of the writing life with motherhood in a similar way to Kim Brooks's 2018 online article for *The Cut*: 'Portrait of the Artist as a Young Mom'. 'Surely there was no reason,' Brooks ponders, 'that a person like myself couldn't be a great wife, a great mother, and also the sort of obsessive, depressive, distracted writer whose persona I'd always romanticized.'

Of course, I sympathise with Brooks. I know how demanding it can be to balance life, work, and children. When she lists the parts of motherhood that she wants to jettison – playdates, birthday parties, parent nights, after-school activities, and worrying about standardised test scores – I am right there with her. But do these ephemeral concerns have to be an inherent part of motherhood? When Brooks rejects the exasperating aspects of parenting, isn't she really describing the demands of bourgeois motherhood, white middle-class motherhood, suburban motherhood?

Because motherhood is not necessarily what Brooks describes, nor does creativity have to be incompatible with domestic life. Once all the consumerist, competitive rubbish is cast off, what is left behind is a more positive way of parenting that demands focus, mindfulness, and awareness of others. It's a way of life that can be inspiring and empowering, but it entails rejecting stereotypes of creativity that are so often defined in terms of men's lives and experiences.

Brooks wants to be a Byron, promiscuous and sensational, or a Baudelaire walking the streets of Paris. She wants to be Verlaine engaging in stormy affairs, or Faulkner refusing his daughter's demands because 'Nobody remembers Shakespeare's children.' The trouble is that all of these personae entail an individualism that cannot be maintained in the life of domesticity and being a good parent. There is something tiresome and distasteful about romanticising these men, who in order to define themselves as marked by genius, led lives that were intrinsically selfish. In Brooks's eyes, being a parent and especially a mother means being 'cautious, boring' and 'conventional.'

But what if we replaced the word 'cautious' with 'mindful'? The word 'boring' with 'repetitive' or 'cyclic'? The word 'conventional' with 'steady'? Because one of the most positive things that has come from motherhood for me is the sense of time and ritual. Before kids, my life worked on the principle of spontaneity – whatever I wanted to do in a particular moment I did. No timetables for me. But as a mother, I have found a new appreciation and mindfulness of the time, the seasons, days passing, and how to schedule and make that time as full and beneficial as I can. I am not talking about the obsessive scheduling

14

of after-school classes, but the joy that children take in the changing of the seasons and weather. What I have found is a more spiritual and mindful life.

Mindfulness is a particularly important word, because children force you to live in the moment too. Like the greedy babies in Clarke's poem, they are hungry for whatever is near them. You find yourself appreciating the food that you eat, the simple walk of an evening through your neighbourhood, the hour that slips by with imagining and play, and falling asleep together after a long day. Such a life is certainly not a bad thing for the artist.

Having lived through unsettling and disturbing experiences, for someone like me maintaining a stable and quiet life is subversive. Like Brooks, I am sentimental about the nobility of suffering: Brooks tells us that 'the point of art is to unsettle', but 'that shouldn't be anyone's goal as a parent.' This is a false problem. When Brooks suggests that 'People make art for exactly the opposite they make families', I ask, why do the projects need to have the same creative energy? Why can't we create a steady family life alongside art that questions and disturbs? Because being in close contact with children, with their vulnerability, openness, and joy, can only bring into focus the wrongness, the dysfunction of the communities in which we live.

On a more practical level, Brooks rightly points out that children are demanding. One mother that Brooks interviews complains how when she is writing, she becomes distracted, and her daughter is resentful. I know exactly what she is talking about, and I sympathise, but I have also found that being forced to come back to the present moment can be positive. Before kids, I used to write with an obsessive intensity, spending whole days and nights lost in whatever I was working on. But now, I have to be present. I have to take breaks, and focus on others, and this is not necessarily a bad thing.

Some of the most productive moments I ever had were when I had to stop writing something so that I could breastfeed my son.

Those quiet moments were incredibly fruitful. It was impossible to write anything down, but I could run over and over any ideas that had settled in my brain. What this means, however, is a different way of working. It means being patient. It means waiting before you write anything down. It means thinking things through carefully, slowly, or using the word that Brooks despises: cautiously.

Having said all this, as a mother, time is my biggest problem. When so much time has to be earmarked for children and the running of domesticity, this is the hard thing. But it is a political issue too, because mothering does not happen in a vacuum, and fathers have a responsibility too to play their part, let alone the issue of access to childcare, and the need for better and equal maternity or paternity leave.

I am not trying to say that combining motherhood and creativity is easy, and in no way do I blame Brooks for the comments she makes. But I do believe that it is possible to make a productive and rich writing life as a mother, and against Brooks's list of women writers troubled by maternity, I would list Toni Morrison, Jhumpa Lahiri, Marilynne Robinson, and Zadie Smith. The point is that we have to try to change expectations: first we must challenge ideas about what mothers do, but we also have to defy stereotypical imaginings of what creativity looks like. The tortured male genius with the sensational life is a dead end: it is not necessarily a productive route to creative success.

In many ways, as a mother, I feel that I am improved, tougher, more resilient, hungry, and determined. In spite of all obstacles, when I do sit down to write, there is no prevaricating, no procrastinating about what is emerging. I know that this might be the only moment I have. There can be no excuses: now is my time to write.

Not *Breakfast at Tiffany's*

An ex of mine once told me I reminded him of Holly Golightly. In fact, he told me I *must* have modelled myself on her. I had only watched the 1961 film *Breakfast at Tiffany's* once, and it annoyed me: the assumption that I was acting out a persona, that I was fake in some way. If I was being honest with myself though, I would have admitted that the film made a big impression on me.

To be honest, I wasn't sure that I lived up to the comparison, but who wouldn't love Audrey Hepburn's Holly Golightly? I watched the film when I was seventeen, and I had just fought my way out of a relationship with an abusive older man. Holly seemed closer to my experience than any other woman I had watched in my teenage years.

Traumatised women on film in the 1980s and 90s were often portrayed as mad, bad, and dangerous to know. Think Shakespeare's Ophelia with a dose of *Fatal Attraction* and *Single White Female* thrown in. Or there were the 'cool girls', a term coined by Gillian Flynn in her novel *Gone Girl*, to describe the women who are always down with the boys. In *Pulp Fiction*, Uma Thurman's cool *femme fatale* overdoses, and has to be brought back to life by a needle through her breastbone straight to the heart. But hey, no worries: she's a cool girl, and the cool girl never struggles, never makes a fuss. In the #metoo moment though, it is easy to see the misogyny of these stories, especially in the light of recent allegations about Quentin Tarantino's abusive practices with actresses.

There were no room in these stories for women like me, but

perhaps I liked Holly because her troubled character just made her more alluring. She is probably closest to another 1990s trope: the manic pixie girl, because she is more eccentric than cool. The object of struggling writer Paul Varjak's thoughtful gaze, Holly is not hysterical, or vicious, as most female victims are framed. Her trauma is signalled when she wakes up screaming in Paul's bed, while later we discover that she was married off to a much older man as a child bride at fourteen, a union that was later annulled. Finally, she loses her brother during his service in the army.

In the film, however, this story comes at the expense of non-white people with Mickey Rooney providing a supposedly 'comic' (in fact objectionable) performance as pernicious stereotype Mr. Yunioshi. The source text too is tinged with racism. In Truman Capote's 1958 novel, when the narrator (Paul) is forced to reminisce about Holly and her long absence, a friend tells him of a wood carving in her exact likeness discovered in an African village. Holly's sexual power is framed by her status as a conquering white woman who supposedly civilises the natives. The story of Holly Golightly is not unproblematic, and white trauma is told at the expense of black and Asian people.

Reconsidering the film now, twenty years after I originally saw it, I question what gave it such power for me as a teenager and recognise its flaws. Perhaps it is simply the idea of becoming another person; Holly changes her accent, her style, and her appearance as if shedding the trauma of a former life. Paul is central to the film's attraction too, a man who understands the experience of being sexually coerced because he relies financially on a wealthy lover. Despite knowing Holly's difficult past and her arguably subversive present as what Truman Capote called 'an American Geisha', Paul hardly ever judges her, except at the end of the film when he challenges her not to leave him, but to settle down, and live a heteronormative, conventional love story.

The novel is more subversive, because it refuses the film's conventional ending, and it makes Holly much more than a 1990s

Manic Pixie Girl. Nathan Rabin, one of the first writers to coin the term, Manic Pixie Girl (MPG) in an article for *AV Film*, complained that the MPG existed 'solely in the fevered imaginations of sensitive writer-directors to teach broodingly soulful young men to embrace life and its infinite mysteries and adventure.' Holly is far more inspiring and independent in Capote's novel, where the characters never know what happened to Holly, but speculate as to whether she might be dead, in an asylum, or settled down to marry at last. The uncertainty is significant because it allows Holly her privacy and her freedom: she has her own story beyond Paul.

Flawed as it was, I loved *Breakfast at Tiffany's* at seventeen, but perhaps only because the models of women survivors were so poor that Holly was the only figure of trauma I could turn to, one of the few women onscreen to whom I could in my imagination at least say #metoo. Women who now turn to the #metoo movement deserve better models for routes out of self-blame and self-destruction, better narratives through which to realise that survival is possible.

Just a Woman with Nothing on Her Skin

What are the politics of a photograph? Legally, the photograph belongs to the photographer. But how does this dynamic play out when so often women and minorities have been the erotic spectacle of photographs, whether they consent or not? This article is not about changing copyright rules, but it does recall Laura Mulvey's essay 'Visual Pleasure and Narrative Cinema', and her statement that 'In a world ordered by sexual imbalance, pleasure in looking has been split between active/male and passive/female.'

In my poetry collection, *Hand & Skull*, the photograph becomes an important way to explore power, sexuality, violence, and healing. At the heart of this discussion is a series of photographs: Alfred Stieglitz's images of the artist, Georgia O'Keeffe. During the 1910s, Stieglitz was a photographer and key influencer on the New York art scene, and he and O'Keeffe went on to have a prolific correspondence, their letters leading to a passionate attachment, and eventually their marriage.

I first came across Stieglitz's photographs in a book of postcards: a Christmas present when I was about thirteen. It was a picture of Georgia O'Keeffe's hands: almost disembodied, lying on a bed of sumptuous material. The finger and thumb of one hand delicately hold a needle, while on the other hand, the middle finger is languorously extended, and capped by a thimble. I was very young, but the photograph meant something to me: spoke to me about power, delicacy, physicality, and presence. I carried the postcard around in a notebook for years, until eventually I lost it.

Years later, in New York, I saw other images that Stieglitz took of O'Keeffe: a catalogue of her body. Her upturned chin and the lovely bones of her clavicle. Her face pensive, fingers clutching a coat about her chin. Fingers clasped and balanced on her knees like a schoolgirl. Hands caught in the delicate act of buttoning a coat. Head thrown back, face uplifted, and hair falling down. The back of her head as she twists her hair up into a clip, vulnerable somehow with the neck bare. A soft snapshot of her breasts and stomach.

There is so much that is contradictory about the photographs. They are so beautiful, and they could be empowering as they celebrate an unsanitised version of a woman's body, but there are problems too. Is there something disturbing about how Stieglitz breaks her body down into parts? Isn't it objectifying? And who has the power in this relationship? It is hard to see O'Keeffe as passive, and I can't help wondering if she herself had a strong influence on how the photographs were taken, so that it might not be that she was a passive object, but that the series was collaborative.

There is another potential to the photograph though: something abusive and exploitative. In thinking about O'Keeffe, I couldn't help remembering the times when – in a past abusive relationship – my ex-partner would take photographs of me unexpectedly and without my consent. Who does the photograph belong to in a scenario like this?

In relation to this personal story, we could discuss recent news stories about exploitative or abusive photographers. We could consider examples of celebrities where nude photographs have been released to the public. For the person whose image is being consumed, it is a disturbing experience. I tried to explain this feeling in a social media post, grasping for words to describe how odd it feels to imagine an abusive ex still having a photograph of you, a photo taken without your consent: one man responded by telling me that this was a clichéd idea, and to write about something else.

The problem is that women and minorities often have to bear the brunt of representations beyond their control, and in *Hand & Skull,* alongside the commentary on O'Keeffe and the photograph, I have tried to lift up the voices of women and minorities who sometimes have not had a say in how they are looked at, viewed, or represented. There is the voice, for example, of Emily Doe, survivor of the 2016 'Stanford Swimmer' rape case, and also voices from Amnesty International's 'Stonewalled' report on police abuses of LGBT (and especially BAME) people in the US.

Georgia O'Keeffe's and Alfred Stieglitz's collaboration is wonderful but also thought-provoking. O'Keeffe initially seems to accept Stieglitz's idealising of her as an archetypal and essentialist woman, but eventually they drifted apart in their marriage, and O'Keeffe found more sustenance, and freedom, in the American West. Despite this, they continued to keep up a correspondence as documented in the moving volume *My Faraway One.* Out West, O'Keeffe comes into her own, and she describes to Stieglitz from Canyon, Texas the act of looking in a mirror: 'I saw myself as I have, often – dropping my clothes in the morning – standing there screwing my hair up tight before going to the bathroom – just a woman with nothing on her skin': a woman in command of her own image at last.

Turtle Hatching

The first time I had a miscarriage, it was 'missed'. Sometimes they call it a silent miscarriage, because there are no symptoms. The only time you find out is when you lie back to have the ultrasound, but instead of a baby, nothing is there.

A friend of mine who miscarried used to comfort herself by looking at it logically. She compared the act of giving birth to the passage of baby sea turtles from an egg buried under the sand to the open sea. Not all the baby turtles survive, but some do. I respect the fact that the thought gave her comfort, but it is still hard to think of small things dying.

I am writing this in the aftermath of my fourth miscarriage. I am back at home after having a D&C at the hospital, and my husband is out collecting our two kids from school. It's my sixth pregnancy but only two out of the six have survived: this last one didn't make it.

I keep thinking about the dreams. First, I dreamed the foetus's name, and before I knew the sex, I dreamed I was taking a baby girl home to Wales to my grandmother's house: the house which has belonged to our family for a hundred years. The foetus was a female, but something was wrong: in a later dream, I lost my youngest son in the complex of a swimming pool. When I began to question if all was well, the final answer came to me in a dream: the doctor giving me an ultrasound said, 'The baby is in the wrong place.' The dreams were trying to tell me what had happened, because the body knows things about itself even when you are not exactly conscious of it.

It happened the first time I miscarried too. Though my body and mind missed the miscarriage when it happened, there was one peculiar sign. In the weeks before we found out, a particular song was stuck in my head – 'She's Leaving Home' by the Beatles. It tells the story of a daughter who leaves the wretched conformist life set out by her parents, but after she has gone her mother, crying, calls out for 'Daddy', telling him: 'our baby's gone.' The song stuck in my head was a kind of displacement, or what in literary studies we call metonymy, where meaning is placed onto something adjacent to what you really want to talk about. This was my mind's peculiar way of trying to communicate. I now really hate this song, though I know it's not logical.

You never get used to having a miscarriage, and very often people say the wrong thing though they mean well. 'Nature has a plan' is not very comforting. 'They happen to everybody' does not really signify when it is happening to you. Sometimes people will tell you 'You'll have another one soon enough' or 'At least you already have children.' But they fail to recognise how monumental it feels to lose even one, or how fragile any predictions for the future must be.

Meanwhile, friends are writing telling me how brave I am for being so open about my miscarriage. I don't feel very brave, but I do refuse to be silenced by shame. Talking to my friend, poet So Mayer, I suggest the idea of writing *against* shame, and they gently correct me, offering instead the idea of writing with/through shame, because 'writing against anything produces and centres it.'

There are so many things that women (and childbearing people) do not know before becoming pregnant. We aren't told that though our bodies may contain life, they can also contain death. We are sold the idea of the blissful pregnant woman who glows with ease, when the body is so fragile, and it is miracle that anyone is born at all. We do not know about the unsympathetic medical system which very often belittles mothers' choices and wishes, and especially in the case of black people, ignores their pain. We are not told how some people reduce our humanity to a vessel, carrying a life thought to have more importance than our own.

This is why I would fight for the rights of any woman (or non-binary person) to *not* have to be mothers. Because the US has the highest rate of mother mortalities in the Western world. Because though giving birth can be humbling and incredible, it is also a physical, bodily effort which involves pain of many different kinds.

Somehow in writing this, I have moved from the sadness I feel about the miscarriages to the right of people not to be pregnant. The way I see it though, it is all bound up, because both are a source of anxiety for Western culture. What do they do with the woman who miscarries, or with the woman who chooses not to have a baby at all? It's time that we rewrite the stereotypes without shame or blame: new stories that admit the precarity of life, and the labour that goes into creating it.

II. Power and the State

Sense of an ending.

Notes from a Swing State

I. The Day of the Election, November 8ᵗʰ 2016

I am driving home from work. The sun is setting. Did I tell you that we have the most incredible skies in Ohio? I couldn't get used to it at first. I grew up in a town in Wales, where the sky is a flat lid and the valley bends round like cupped and comforting hands. But here, the sky is a down-turned bowl, and we are so small underneath it.

Anyway, I am driving home, and the sky is reddening, great slashes of white from vapour trails, and flaming trees like torches. I am listening to a sad song on the radio, and I feel as though something is ending. Like sitting in an empty house when someone you love has closed the door behind them with no possibility of return.

A few weeks earlier, I am canvassing for Hillary Clinton. I am driving round my neighbourhood with Sandra, a white nurse from a biracial family who is worried about her son. We have a list of addresses where the occupants voted Democrat in past elections. We knock doors and they open onto people saying, *I am so glad to see you*; the warmth so palpable: as if they might hold us in their arms, they are so afraid.

One house is at the end of a long drive, trees and pastures all around, and there, with his back to us, a bearded man sits cross-legged on the ground whittling a piece of wood, a chainsaw lying beside him.

Sandra walks towards the man, her slim, tidy figure buffeted by the breeze. He continues to sit, his bulk on the ground, his eyes on the wood.

29

Sandra asks him if he is voting for Clinton.

He says, *No, I can't stand Hillary. I can't say how much I hate her*. Sandra warns him that he runs the risk of a Trump presidency.

He doesn't care, he despises Hillary so much. *She wants power too much*, he says.

Sandra asks if she can turn the car around in his drive, and when we pull into the yard, all the windows are blanketed, but the corner of a face emerges at the edge: just a pair of dark eyes and a wisp of hair.

Someone else lives here too, I say, looking at my list. *A woman*.

2. The Day of the Attack, November 28th 2016

It has crossed my mind, of course. When I begin teaching a new class, I check out the room, look for viable exits, and consider how I would secure the room. When a campus police officer trained the department in emergency protocol, she told us to *Run, hide, fight*. But many of the classroom doors are impossible to lock. *The people who do these things*, she tells us, *they aren't superheroes. If the worst comes to worst, you have a good chance of taking them down if you work together.*

But when the worst does happen, I am sat at home, watching the university shutdown via rolling news. There's the car park I use being stormed by a SWAT team. The building I walk by each day is sealed off by tape. There is the spot where Abdul Razak Arkan ran down a crowd with his car, got out and started slashing with a butcher knife.

He was interviewed a few months before for *Humans of Ohio State*. He told the interviewer that he was afraid to pray in the open. *I don't know what is going to happen if I do*, he said.

The next day I am teaching. One student begins to cry. I tell the class that life is random, that we cannot anticipate what is coming next. I tell them: please, look out for our Somali students. I tell them that they have to be prepared.

On Campus Today mails out counselling resources. I think of students I taught in the past. The ones who took Alertec to work

30

for forty-eight hours straight. Some with anxiety attacks. Others that cracked under the pressure and just stopped coming to class, not even a goodbye.

3. Post-Election

Comparisons Brexit

After the election, I find myself looking at familiar faces with suspicion and unease. Is my child's teacher a Trump supporter? My doctor?

The woman behind the counter at my morning coffee shop wears a hijab. My husband blurts out that I canvassed for Clinton. The woman looks relieved.

I wonder if I should start wearing a safety pin to show people that I am an ally. A friend of mine writes to me that safety pins are lame. *I can't take off my race like a safety pin*, she says.

News is circulating on Facebook, and if I read it before bed, I have trouble sleeping. Almost as though they sense the trouble, the children start climbing into bed in the middle of the night, their small, knobbly bodies nuzzling in, and I hold them very close.

At night, I revisit the women I have written about. From Welsh myth, Blodeuwedd, the woman of flowers, created by a magician for the pleasure of men: how she fought against it, followed her own desire, became an owl under the cover of night. From Central America, La Malinche, who lived her life as a slave of one kind or another, no choice except to survive as best she could, even as the woman of a Conquistador. From America, Tamzene Donner, a colonist going west, caught by snow in the Hastings Cutoff: the party reduced to cannibalism, she stayed behind with her dying husband. Even if they did not exactly succeed, these women faced the worst, and suddenly, I am far more certain.

We are writing letters here, writing postcards, contacting politicians, applying pressure. We are using pen and paper or the telephone, because online petitions are ignored. We are marching on capital buildings. We are rallying in our lunchtimes, squeezing in protests around schoolwork and children's bedtimes. We are

31

donating equipment and warm clothes to the people of Standing Rock. But we have to refuse. We have to say no. We have to stand up for each other. This is the only option. There is no other choice.

4. 14 May 2019

Today abortion will be banned in Alabama, but I won't know that it has happened until late at night. Lying in bed, I will check the blue light of my cellphone. We are all waiting for the next election, but nobody knows what will happen.

Meanwhile, I walk the woods of our neighbourhood, and notice a beetle that has landed on my hand. I watch it crawl over my finger, before it pauses. It bites me, and without thinking, I flick it away with my thumb. I wonder if the beetle is trying to tell me something about the futility of kindness. How strange it is: these suburban people, walking around and telling themselves how kind and good they are, despite immigrant children torn from their mothers: despite the slow erosion of the rights of queer folx: despite the hard, bright voices talking about money, and God, and the good old days.

How can it be that they once were babies, curling their tiny fingers, opening their tiny mouths for food? Nothing is more frightening to Americans than dependence. The headlines are shouting it. One politician accepts eggs destroyed by fertility clinics, by the white-coated men of his imagination, but not those aborted, because it terrifies him: that woman might have power over their own bodies. Another describes pregnant women as hosts, because he is so afraid of the idea that he was once part of his mother's body, that deep in the womb he was connected, not separate.

The Buddhists believe in dependent origination, or the idea that nothing happens that has not been caused by something else, and that each event goes on to ripple out with multitudes of consequences. I am thinking about this as I watch a great yellow butterfly hovering above the weeds, dancing and dancing over the leaves, never quite touching the ground.

The Missing Line

A girl sits on the edge of the platform. She is at the far end, a little apart from the crowds of children on the station, and her legs hang off the platform edge. She is wearing a thick coat over her grammar school uniform, a beret on the back of her head. In her gloved hands is a square, green, cardboard ticket. Her legs are covered by woollen tights, but the cold from the stone platform is inching through her skirt.

By now, her Mama will be out with the peroxide bottle, dying hair, or papering the walls of a neighbour's house, and Dada will be back from his night shift at St John's Pit. He will be sleeping back at home. She knows he would hate to see her legs dangling off the platform, but before long she hears the rails hissing, and scrambles up as the long, juddering bulk of the train pulls into view, steam clouding the frosty air.

The children tumble onto the train when it pulls in, shrieking in the compartments, and the girl gets on too. As the doors slam, and the train begins to heave away, she pushes down a window and leans out into the cold air, leans out carefully to avoid the coke carried on smoke from the engine.

It's not a true story, just a moment as I imagine it from 1961, and the girl is my mother catching the train down the valley to grammar school, the first in her family to make it that far. She tells me how it was, when I call her from Ohio: from Columbus where you are never too far from a railway crossing, and at night you hear the freight trains hooting and whistling through your sleep. The

33

passenger trains in America are mainly defunct – too expensive or too slow for the majority. Road, not rail, is the American dream.

In my family home, the Llynfi valley, passenger trains were almost closed down forever. They ended in 1970, though the long freights of coal continued. The route wasn't reinstated until the 1990s, and then only to Maesteg, while further up the valley the rails turned to rust.

My mother is talking on the phone about what the train meant. 'It took you,' she says, 'to the places we didn't normally see. Just a stone's throw away, out there on the train, it was all green and wild.'

It is really my mother's story: telling about the Maesteg line, and the twenty-first century is a poor time to tell its story. It's true that a passenger train scoots up and down the line from Maesteg to Bridgend and back, but it's a ghost of what it used to be. Anything is an improvement on the twenty years when there were no passenger trains at all.

The station at Llangynwyd for my mother's grammar school no longer exists, closed by Dr. Beeching in the 1960s. Travelling up the valley, the line ends at Maesteg, but rails half covered by weeds still lead up through Nantyfyllon to Caerau. The tunnel where the train once passed to Cymmer collapsed from neglect, and overgrown lines trace a path to the empty spaces where collieries used to be. My grandfather, my great-grandfather – all the men in my family – spent years of their lives digging coal, much later to die of pneumoconiosis or pneumonia. My grandfather after his nightshift would sit in the kitchen barrel-chested, his eyelashes rimmed with coal dust like mascara, and the coal in the cuts on his fingers left vivid blue-green tracks under the skin, familiar to those from mining families.

Now the knotweed, once planted to fend off the erosion of railway banks, invades the gardens of terraced houses. After living in the Rhondda valley, my Basque friend, Marta, told me that one of the greatest injustices to the valley people was the lack of a high-speed rail link to Cardiff. 'It just strikes me some places in the

34

valleys can feel so cut off. When the transport links came to Bilbao,' she explains, 'we prospered and grew. It enabled social mingling, and social mobility. We worked in the city by day, but then we went back to our homes. Our towns were no longer islands. It made us freer.'

Such a project seems unlikely if not unthinkable in a region as neglected as Wales, and so we cling to what little we have.

One night, on my summer visit to Wales, I take the last train back to Maesteg. I am standing by the door of the carriage, trying to make out shapes in the dark air, when a man stumbles forward. He asks if we have reached Tondu, a little station at the bottom of the valley.

'That's it,' he says. 'I'm getting out at Tondu.' A friend appears at his side saying:

'Not Tondu! We talked about this. We agreed you weren't going to do this again. You said you'd just leave it.'

'No,' replies the man staggering a little. 'It's Tondu for me. It's no good trying to stop me.'

And I can't help wondering what temptations Tondu might hold. Sex? Booze? Drugs? When we do reach Tondu, a few revellers get on still holding their pint glasses, and they carry on their conversations as if they were still in the pub lounge.

There's more on an afternoon trip when I catch the train again from Bridgend. On the map, the straight railway line runs alongside the River Llynfi tangling this way and that, snarling like string around a metal wire. The Llynfi, a river that nearly died after the mining era, abiotic until it was nursed back to health, but it did come back, just like slag heaps have grown over green, and there is little to mark the spot where the dark, spidery pitheads once stood.

On the outskirts of Maesteg, the embankments build to a hump: a long spine of earth along the bottom of the valley. From up there, the train looks down on the town: the long red terraces, the backs of houses like shy faces, and yards full of flowers and children's toys. The pointed spires and coronets of churches remain: Bethel, Bethania, and Bethlehem; Zion, and Shiloh; St Michaels and All the Angels; Our Lady and St. Patrick. Above it all, Garth Mountain hulks like a great, faceless animal, brooding and sublime.

Perhaps this is what the train does for us here too. When we travel by rail, we can really look for a change; can gaze at the wild green spaces that surround our town like a nest. Travelling with pushchairs and briefcases, backpacks and pint glasses, we are carried up and through the valley, and as we go about our work, our conversations, our duties and laughter, we can see the town unfolding, the concerns of the houses and town small under the shadow of the mountains: Garth, and Pwll-y-lwch.

I want to save this moment that my mother describes: leaning out of the train window; the train pulling out of the town; the wind rushing around her ears: exhilarating and chill. Beyond the houses and yards, the forest is thickening. Mist clouds the trees, and ice hangs like lacework on the branches. How she feels it then: riding on the engine's thundering clatter, gliding through the silence of trees, and faraway on the mountain, the sheep run in fright without making a sound.

The Heaven Girls and Murder Alley: A Family Story

The last time I saw my English grandmother, she seemed paper-thin. She is nearly ninety now, and last Christmas I travelled back to Britain from my home in Ohio just to see her, because the nurses had told us that she was losing the will to keep going, that she seemed to be slipping away. I visited the nursing home every day of that trip, holding on to her fingers, shiny and smooth like something worn clean by the sea. There was carol singing, a choir conducted by a lady with a walking stick in a tweed skirt like a character from Daphne du Maurier's novel *Rebecca*.

My father's family is from Bristol, and as a child, they held a certain fascination for me. My parents separated when I was four, and I grew up with my Welsh family for the most part, only seeing the English side once or twice a year. I would go there in the summer holidays, and it was all as idyllic as a postcard, or a town from an Agatha Christie novel (but without the murder). There was lemon meringue pie with crisp, sugary bergs; afternoons in the garden trimming the roses and the edges of the lawn; or daytrips to the downs, the great hot air balloons lazing in the sky, or kites quivering mid-air. My grandfather would wash up the dishes so carefully, and we would listen to records in the evening and play cards. Sometimes, we would visit Aunty Pauline up at Windy Ridge, and the fruit trees were so heavy that the ground would be carpeted with apples.

My grandfather died many years ago from Parkinson's Disease, and now my grandmother is in a nursing home in a pretty town outside Bristol. She is getting the sharp look that comes to elderly people late in life, and she seems to find it harder to remember things, but despite all that, her quick intelligence and laughter are still there.

One day I am on the phone to her from America, and I tell her about the deep, thick, lovely snow that is covering everything here through the winter. I tell how my son and I are out building a snowman, how my son keeps throwing snowballs at me, until at last, I beckon to him: 'Come here,' I say. 'I have something to show you.' He walks over curiously – he is always so curious – and before he knows it, out of my hand comes the cold shock of a snowball right in his face.

'You didn't?' says my grandmother.

'I did,' I reply.

'That reminds me,' she says, and she begins to tell me. It was when they lived out at Long Ashton, before they moved into the city. One day when she was a little girl, the snow had arrived. She saw children playing outside the cottage window, and stuck her head through to say hello. She must have looked striking with her head of red hair, and some boy threw a snowball at her face. That was enough for my grandmother: on with her boots and coat, and out she went to get revenge. By the time she had finished with him he was wet all over, and his mother called to complain that his shirt was soaking, and to tell my great-grandmother to rein in that Rita Heaven girl.

As a young woman, my grandmother worked as a photographer's assistant in Clifton in Bristol, and she must have been daring because she had her photograph taken in a bikini for the window display, to entice other young women to come and do the same.

Clifton is Bristol's beautiful white city on the hill, its tall white buildings, elegant windows, tasteful scrollwork, its market, and boutique shops and restaurants. Of course, it might as well be built out of bone, because the wealth there came from the slave trade,

38

blood money from plantations in the Caribbean. The faraway bodies of black slaves built the magical city.

But working in Clifton, how glamorous my grandmother must have seemed to my grandfather, James Brigley, whose family lived and worked not at the top of the hill, but at the bottom. His family lived on Waters Place, described in the 1900s as notorious for crime and poverty, with houses that shared toilets and water supply. Nine people living in one room was not uncommon. It was even known for a time as 'Murder Alley'. During their time there, three of my grandfather's siblings died: Frederick died at age two, Lillian at seven, and Walter at four. It is a devastating catalogue of loss, and ultimately the only children to survive were my grandfather (the youngest), and his two much older sisters, who had grown up before entering the squalor of Waters Place.

But how did the family end up here? My great-grandfather, Frederick Brigley, was a railway porter, disinherited from a military family of Royal Engineers, because he was a bastard. The Brigley family began as printers in Dublin, but before long became mapmakers for British empire-building in Egypt and Palestine, tracing the roads and bridges that would provide the infrastructure for the colonial project. It is difficult to find out anything about Frederick's mother, Florence, but the family story goes that she was in service with a rich family, and once there was coerced into sex by one of the men of the house. There is no way of knowing who the father was, and Florence, disowned, was alone until she managed to marry. She died in her thirties when Frederick was only fifteen. She left her son a gift, however: her father's name: Frederick Brigley. Despite the fact that her son was born out of wedlock, she named the baby after her father 'Frederick', and insisted on keeping the surname Brigley. This act of love by a mother for her son – this defiance of illegitimacy – is the reason why I bear this peculiar surname today.

The family inheritance of shame was strong for my grandfather James. He was too young to remember the deaths of his siblings, but it must have embittered his father Frederick, who also had the appalling task of serving in the Royal Artillery during World War One. When I ask my grandmother about Frederick, she only remembers him as a cruel and bitter man, someone she sought to avoid. James went into the army after World War Two, travelling British colonies, like Belize. Eventually, he married my grandmother, and became a manager at a chocolate factory in Bristol. Life must have seemed idyllic then, with his neat house bought from the council, and the rose garden that he prized.

There is a family story about an argument they had: how coming back from a dinner at the house of some affluent friends, my grandfather accused my grandmother of wanting 'things' that he could not give her. There was a siege-like war in the house, my grandmother even worrying to my father – then a small boy – that her husband did not love them anymore, and my grandfather disappearing to the shed every free moment. But then something happened: he came out of the shed and along with him he brought something he had made. Like in all family stories, the details are hazy: it might have been a chair or table, but what was important was that all that time he had been labouring, carving, joining, as if the work itself was on him and her, or perhaps to make himself more perfect in her eyes: not the boy from Waters Place.

But my grandfather underestimated how much my grandmother loved him: doubt was his inheritance. Her life had not been perfect before she met him, even if she was not as poor. Her parents divorced when she was a child, and they were exiled from their house at Long Ashton. Even now, she remembers vividly the crinkling of the bags that held their meagre belongings, and the gravel's crunch under her shoes, as her mother, brother, and sisters walked away. It was World War Two then, and Bristol was not safe. It was the time when her fainting began. My grandmother's famous dizzy spells began on a night when German war planes were dropping bombs over Bristol, whole houses blown to bits, and shrapnel was raining down on the leaves of the allotments. In the morning, at the end of my grandmother's garden, there was a huge crater just metres from the house.

That day when I am talking to my grandmother about the snow, she makes a slip of the tongue, and instead of saying, 'When the snow came,' she says, 'When the war came.' She stops and corrects herself, but it is a thought-provoking mistake, as if war fell over the land like a blanket of ice. We like to think of the World War Two generation as the best generation, and it is easy to see why, but it is worth remembering that the trauma of war did not evaporate. It remained like my grandmother's fainting spells. And trauma was not only felt in foreign wars, but at home in a class system that held no regard for the deaths of my grandfather's infant siblings, or in the false morality that saw the rest of the empire-building Brigleys disown a child just because it was born out of wedlock. It is so easy and quick: the slip from life to death, from comfort to poverty. This my grandparents knew, and they tried to carve out for themselves a tiny life of safety and shelter.

My grandmother is still trying to do this in the routines and quiet of the nursing home. Because her heart cannot be operated on, her days are numbered, but I hope that they will number many. She has admitted to me that at times she is afraid of dying, and she complains about old age. When I look at her now, she seems very small, like a button at the bottom of a well or the last trembling leaf on a branch, but she is still so vivid. She is still the red-headed girl who soaked the rude boy with snow: still Miss Heaven: still the long-legged beauty who posed in her swimsuit: still the flaming Rita-Hayworth-lookalike who turned my grandfather's head all those years ago.

Life on Mars

When I heard that David Bowie died, the first thing I did was pull up YouTube. I focussed on hearing the songs again, and let the chaos of the morning at our house – plastic spoons, bibs, toy trucks – unfurl around me. When I first listened to 'Life on Mars?', I just heard a great song: the children wailed along to *sailors fighting in the dance hall*, spinning round the kitchen, and swinging to the beat.

Later I listened again, with nobody else in the kitchen. Tiny spots of snow were falling on the other side of the glass doors, and my hand was cramped with the cold. I was trying to work out why the song was so important, and I remembered listening to Bowie for the very first time. I had an ugly black box of a cassette player, and I was seventeen.

Commenting in the 70s on the story of 'Life on Mars?', Bowie said that the song imagined a 'sensitive young girl' and her reaction to the media: a media that promised a beautiful dream of a life but did not deliver. How fresh and raw it was then for my seventeen-year-old self still half-dreaming of the perfect heterosexual romance, and feeling cheated beyond belief. How bitter and old I felt too, and each romantic silver-screen image like a pale imitation of a starker truth.

Bowie himself probably committed statutory rape, and so it is ironic that, fifteen years after writing 'Life on Mars?', he could reach a troubled seventeen-year-old and make her feel powerful and wise. Bowie is tainted by the allegations. Nothing can make up for that. Nothing should silence that fact. But then Bowie wasn't joking when he asked us to be heroes just for one day. Bowie was an artist, not a hero, and he knew it, or perhaps we should have known that uncomplicated heroes are a figment of the imagination too.

I don't write this down to excuse Bowie, far from it. Instead, we have to face the unpalatable fact that it is not only monsters that rape, and the men who rape are not simply monstrous. They are friends and colleagues and neighbours. They are comedians and patriarchs and the directors of your favourite films. They are the stars you idolise and adore. In short, rape culture is in the fabric of our very society. Rape culture is the elephant in the room that we are trying to ignore, so we try distraction. When Bowie asks 'Is there life on Mars?,' he flags up a ridiculous and pathetic attempt to look out into the cosmos when we should be looking in at ourselves.

Fuck Self Help

Because I work and teach on domestic violence, people sometimes write to me unexpectedly with their own stories. They are usually women (although abuse does happen to men and non-binary folx too), and often they have questions about whether a partner's behaviour is abusive. Very often it is.

Sometimes these can be liberating stories. A woman once wrote to say that finally, after ten years of an abusive relationship, she had left, and her life had changed irrevocably. Food was more flavoursome, smells were more vivid, colours luminous, as if she had been imprisoned in a grey world.

Other stories are less comforting. I spent a month writing back and forth with a friend on Facebook living in another country. Her abusive boyfriend had dumped her, except she wasn't really dumped: it was more a test to see how much she would put up with before he took her back. We talked many times about working to forget him, and to create a new life. Then one day on Facebook, she posted a photograph of the two of them relaxing at a beachfront hotel. She stopped writing to me then, and while I hope that she is happy, I can't help thinking about what I could or should have done to help her.

I never blamed my friend, but people do criticise victims who go back to abusive partners. I've even had students in class ask, *Why don't they just leave? Why don't they help themselves?* When I say, *Fuck self help*, I'm not talking about people in general who try to better themselves. It's a very specific 'fuck you' to the isolation imposed on victims of intimate partner violence. It's a 'fuck you' to the demand that they leave, while the rest of us continue as if nothing happened.

When Rihanna continued to have a relationship with Chris Brown after he abused her, there was a palpable backlash, despite the fact that people were listening to his music again and the media message demanded that she forgive him. If we don't present real consequences for abusing intimate partners, then how is the victim who is exploited, manipulated, and controlled by that abuser supposed to let go? More often we punish victims for what is perceived as making a fuss, or for failing to move on.

I know how difficult it is to forget an abusive partner, because I had one. I was only eighteen, at university, not comfortable away from home, a ghost floating through an unfamiliar world. Every insecurity I had, he pinpointed, and exploited. It didn't feel like abuse at first, more like having a perfect lover: protective, encouraging, passionate, strong. But how easily those words transform to controlling, manipulative, obsessive, violent.

Like my friend on Facebook, I too went travelling with my boyfriend, at a time when the violence was ratcheting up. We were backpacking through Turkey, the dynamic between us tense at best. He accused me of wanting to leave him, and carry on the trip with a group of Australian men we talked to. One day, he pushed me against the bathroom wall and began to strangle me.

I only have one photograph of us on that trip, taken in Istanbul at the Topkapi Palace, where we spent the afternoon passing through the gates, between two fairytale spires, through gorgeous pavilions and corridors tiled in red and blue, leafed with gold. What surprises me about the photograph is how happy I look, basking in the glow of that charisma he had: how funny and theatrical he could be. I can't help noticing his hand on my shoulder, fingers curled around at the base of the neck.

It was not long after that when we went to the Turkish Baths. The name was in gold over the narrow door, CAĞALOĞLU HAMAMI, and inside was an enclosed courtyard around a marble fountain, with floor upon floor of wooden doors in neat rows.

That evening we were allowed in together. Men and women are

normally separated, but maybe they bent the rules for tourists. We lay there sweating, almost naked together, until the giant of a masseur led me to the fountain. I sat still while he scaled the dead skin from my body with a huge mitt. For a moment, I caught my lover looking at me. I knew that he was feeling something tender, just as I did for him when he sat like a child and let the masseur do his work.

I wonder now if he felt that tenderness as weakness. Perhaps that was why the night ended with him punching me in the street in front of passers by. *You mean nothing to me, nothing. I just don't love you anymore.* He was shaking me in the hotel lobby as we got into the elevator. The man at the desk came up to our room to 'check everything is OK', and I told him nothing, but I promised myself it would be the last time.

When I went home, the university (especially my department) supported me, used emergency funds to move me into new accommodation, and we were kept in separate classes, but our mutual friends peeled away one by one. For them, it was too inconvenient, too awkward, or too uncomfortable to navigate the possibility of a friend – a funny, charismatic, talented friend – being an abuser. They didn't respect my wishes, but brought him along with them to parties and events, or they just fell out of sight, and left me to struggle on my own.

We are very far away from restorative justice, and one reason is politeness: the desire not to interfere in other people's relationships. In most cases, victims are deeply in love with their abusers, a love exacerbated by dependency, and by the exploitation of vulnerabilities. *This is not weakness*, but it is a dangerous situation for victims, and no simple self-help is adequate to solve the problem. Fuck self help. They deserve more *from us*. And not just in the days following an escape, but a month later, six months later, a year later. Even if they go back. A door that stands open for as long as it takes.

Fright House

Americans may have no identity
but they do have wonderful teeth
Baudrillard

It's happening again. As the nights draw in, as trees redden their leaves, as the sweltering of summer's end breaks like a fever: it's election time in Ohio. Two years after President Trump's victory, now we have the US midterms. After the last election, I promised myself that I would collect the husband and kids, and take off during the next election season, but that is a luxury we cannot afford. We cannot afford to take the time from work, but we also cannot afford not to be here to help, because although we don't yet have a vote, we can't turn away from the political race either.

It is a few weeks or so before Halloween, with midterm elections due to fall on November 6th. I am scrolling through ideas for a Halloween party at my kids' school, and reading the news that left-leaning millionaire George Soros has found a pipe-bomb in his mailbox. I am trying to carve out time to canvas for our local Democratic candidate for state senate, Louise Valentine, texting as I drop the kids at school.

—Can you make Saturday?

—How about Sunday?

—Maybe Tuesday but definitely before Halloween.

Later I ask my husband Dan why the elections are so close to the holiday. 'They weren't thinking about Halloween,' he says, 'more the changing seasons. It's been around since agricultural times I guess. Halloween is the end of the harvest season, and so people would be free to travel and vote.' That's the logical conclusion, but I know he is thinking the same as me: that there is something peculiar about American Halloween.

Halloween is a big deal in the US. In the local store, you can buy six-foot inflatable ghosts, tombstones for the garden, or vintage style clocks shrieking Edgar-Allen-Poe-style prose. A friend from work decorates her garden, dressing up a dummy as 'zombie Trump,' and etches her garden gravestones with names like 'Women's rights' or 'Freedom of the Press'.

Kids going trick-or-treating can be cute, but the adults are creepier, especially the men in masks. One of the first times that I took my kids trick-or-treating, a man answered a door in a rubber mask of melted face, flesh burned to molten wax. Another time I am in a Halloween store looking for costume ideas for the kids, when a figure masked like the killer in the movie Halloween jumps out from behind a display: 'Need any help?' I drop my cellphone and the screen shatters. A saleswoman intervenes: 'Sorry, hon. He's only worked here a week. I told him before. He's not supposed to wear the merchandise.' He is still standing there in the mask, as if waiting for something, and I am not looking at him, because if I do, I'm afraid I will give myself away. Because I *am* terrified, but I am not going to show it. He takes off the mask at last, and underneath is a fifteen-year-old white boy.

I do my own kind of trick-or-treating. With an information pack on Democrat, Louise Valentine, I am knocking on doors. Her branding is a red, white, and blue V that might also be a heart, and her slogan is to put people first. She is running on a campaign to improve public schools against a Trump-in-training, Andrew Brenner, who described public education as 'socialism', and suggested privatising schools.

On the doorstep rounds, there are the usual suspects: the Democrat huggers, the we-already-voted-by-mailers, the not-today-thankyous, but something is a little different. At one house,

48

I ask to talk to the family's nineteen-year-old daughter, and a white man, presumably her father, slams the door in my face. At another house, a white man yanks the door open while I am talking to his partner, and he says to me: 'It's time for you to leave. I don't have to listen to this.' The woman turns to him, saying: 'This is my conversation.' She comes out onto the porch, closes the door on the man behind her. I say that I didn't mean to disturb her on a Sunday, that I am fitting in volunteering around my work and kids. She tells me that she used to volunteer too, years ago when she was in college. When I leave, I am wondering what the consequences will be when she goes back into the house to face the man she closed the door on.

At last, it's the week of Halloween, and the news is horrifying. In Kentucky, a white man has a plan to attack a black church, but unable to enter, he shoots two people – Maurice Stallard and Vickie Jones – in a nearby supermarket. In Pittsburgh, another white man attacks the 'Tree of Life' synagogue with an assault rifle and hand-gun, killing eleven people.

Meanwhile, in Ohio, the local news describes outrage at a local 'swastika night' at the Haunted Hoochie, a fright house near Columbus. Every year, the theme park/haunted house provides the opportunity to witness simulations of the most appalling violence, acted out for attendees' amusement. *USA Today* reported in 2015 that the fright house had a dummy head of President Obama mounted on the wall, projected scenes from 9/11, and that actors simulated suicide, and violence against pregnant women. In the *USA Today* report, one of the actors at Haunted Hoochie talked about one display of an upside-down, black and white American flag, like the protest flags sometimes carried by the far-right. 'We're seeing our rights taken away in this country and it's not right,' the zombie-playing actor said. 'We're not going anywhere.'

Now, after a blatant anti-Semitic attack, Haunted Hoochie offers up the chance to wear swastikas to the peanut-crunching

49

crowd. And what does that mean? Do some Ohioans really enjoy this violence? Is a secret desire to witness a far-right dystopia worming away inside them like an itch that needs to be scratched?

Jean Baudrillard once wrote that Disneyland was the theme park that hid a vital truth. That America itself was the theme park, showground of capitalism, and the glitz of the free economy. But what if a better analogy for America is the fright house? The haunted house is a dissimulation: it obscures the fact that America is the real haunted house, the site where anti-Semitic, misogynist, racist and far-right violence are occurring with frightening regularity.

On the night of the elections, I cannot sleep. The children climb into our bed in the early hours as though signalled by an invisible beacon. I check the news: so many women, so many great candidates have won, but Louise Valentine has lost. I commiserate with my neighbour, Julie, who organised volunteering from her dining room table. 'I just don't see it,' she says. 'I don't get why people vote for shitty human beings.'

But perhaps that's the freedom of being in a fright house. The freedom to separate mothers at the border from their children. The freedom to strip the rights of trans people. The freedom to ignore abuses of women, and non-binary people. The freedom to send women who have abortions to prison. The freedom to offend. The freedom to not accept and embrace others. The freedom to live with your fear and anger, and to direct it at others.

The fright house tells us that violence is an illusion, or an act, but the fright house lies. The fright house is America.

Nine Stories with Guns,
and One Without

1.

One day, I am walking to the parking lot to go home, and my path takes me past the Reserve Officers' Training Corps or ROTC, where the university holds programmes for officers in training. I am walking around the back of the building, and I see two men in dress uniform, both holding rifles. One attempts to perform a series of flourishes with his weapon but drops it on the floor.

I walk closer and closer. Logically, I know that the trainee cannot possibly be wielding a loaded weapon, but against all reason, I recognise that I am scared at seeing the guns, and the trainee's incompetence with his weapon. Perhaps it is just that the weapon is present, with the potential to end life instantly.

2.

On October 15th 2018, a man carrying a 12-gauge Mossberg pump shotgun approached a suburban home outside Barron, Wisconsin. Later, he would tell police that he chose this weapon because it 'would inflict the most damage on someone and would most likely be the best choice of shell and weapon to kill someone.'

He hammered on the front door, and when the occupant James Closs, looked out, the man shot him through the stained-glass window. Upstairs, Denise Closs and her thirteen-year-old daughter Jayme were trying to ring 911, but the man shot open the bathroom door before they could make the call. He found the mother holding her daughter in the bathtub, and once the daughter was tied up, he shot the mother too. The whole abduction and the two murders probably took less than ten minutes, though what he didn't know then was that eventually Jayme would escape.

3.

The man who invented the semi-automatic firearm action, David Marshall Williams, was also a convicted murderer, who developed his designs in prison. The 1952 film *Carbine Williams* stars James Stewart as Williams, and in an interview with Dick Simmons, Stewart explained the inventor's success. 'Even in leg irons on the chain gang, Marshall's character stood out ... It should give folks heart, the ones that are down on their luck.'

4.

The Beatles' 'Happiness is a Warm Gun' was purportedly the favourite song of both Paul McCartney and George Harrison on *The White Album*, though there is much debate about what the gun stands for. Is it sex? Drugs?

John Lennon was inspired to write it on seeing the words 'Happiness is a Warm Gun' on the front of a gun magazine. Lennon said of his inspiration: 'I just thought it was a fantastic, insane thing to say. A warm gun means you just shot something.' The article featured a father and son bonding over shooting.

5.

A boy is playing in the park with a pellet gun. The ground is half-covered in snow so he pulls up his hood. He lets off a couple of shots, tucks the toy in his waistband. The bench is cold, but he sits for a few minutes. He just sits for a moment lost in the beauty of it all, watching his breath fog and disappear on the freezing air. A police car pulls up on the grass. Two officers get out holding guns. The boy is not white.

6.

In my son's elementary school, there are regular drills in case of an armed intruder. Outside there is a sign stating that no unauthorised firearms are allowed inside the building, and there is a camera at the door where parents can be buzzed in.

7.

In 2012, after the Sandy Hook school shooting of twenty elementary children, and six adults, I become involved with Moms Demand Action for Gun Sense in America. There is a rally for tougher gun laws outside the civic buildings in Columbus city centre. I take my son with me: he is not much older than eighteen months.

Driving into the city, the roads are packed, but before long it becomes clear that the queues of cars are for 'Disney On Ice', and the pavements are crowded with parents and small children in costume, all making their way to the rink. At the protest, small groups of parents huddle with their kids in hats and coats against the cold. The mayor speaks about how Columbus has been prevented from enacting stricter gun laws because of statewide legislation.

Meanwhile, a group of men in baseball caps and camouflage clothes patrol up and down the other side of the street. They are carrying assault rifles, and one crosses the road. He stands holding his weapon, finger on the trigger, his eyes on the groups of parents and kids.

8.

One of the key moments in the American Western is the reveal of skill with a gun. It is a moment about shame, pride, masculinity, and the right to demand respect by violence. In *Lonesome Dove*, the TV series based on the novel by Larry McMurtry, two captains, Gus McCrae and Woodrow F. Call, walk into a bar, and they order a drink. The barman complains rudely about the dust on the two men's clothes: he calls them 'old timers'. Gus responds by breaking the barman's nose. Gus points a gun to his head, demands the man's 'respect'. He tosses back the whiskey and throws his glass in the air, shoots it to smithereens.

Larry McMurtry writing in the *New York Review of Books* talked about the regular mass shootings in the US, and he found no answers. He described how 'the dead are dead, the wounded are wounded, and except for twenty families, some of them now broken, the violent stream of American life goes on absolutely unchanged. Arizona and indeed America continue to be packed with guns. I own several myself (none of them semi-automatic) and I have no intention of disposing of them, although I don't feel I should conceal them and walk down urban streets.'

9.

In a nearby town, a high school student has been arrested, and charged with inducing panic after threats. Reports tell how students overheard him planning a school shooting, telling how it would be a bloodbath. 'Don't come to school tomorrow.' He held up his backpack with the words: 'I got it in here.'

10.

One year, for a creative writing class, we were studying Sarah Kane's play *Blasted*. It's a violent play, which compares intimate partner violence to the atrocities of world conflicts. In a fantasy version of Britain, which seems to be at war, a reporter, Ian, abuses a young woman in a hotel room, only to have those abuses revisited on him by an anonymous soldier. Before class, one of my students who is in military training wants to talk about the play, and his impressions of it given his experiences.

'It's not realistic,' he tells me. 'Like the scene when the soldier sucks out Ian's eyeballs. I know for a fact that would be really difficult, because on training one of the things we had to do was to suck out a rabbit's eyeballs, and I can tell you it was almost impossible.'

I always hated that scene in *Blasted,* though I understand why Kane includes it: the desire to force middle-class, white audiences to recognise the violence occurring in faraway war zones, the violence at home. And here is a young man sitting in front of me, asked in the course of his training to do something unspeakable. Is he being honest? Is he testing me? Something about him makes me believe that he is telling the truth. Is he marked by what he has done? He is smiling, almost laughing at the grotesqueness of it, as we all might do when faced with something incomprehensible.

'And besides,' he continues. 'You would never need to do something that elaborate if you had a gun in your hand.'

I nod, and we go down to class with this knowledge between us. There is no gun in the classroom, but the shadow of it insists itself between the words we do not say.

1: Photograph by Zoë Brigley, Arches National Park, 2010.

"Arches was not a hostile land exactly, but rocks that had persisted for aeons, and were quite indifferent to human suffering."

2: Photograph by Zoë Brigley, the Delicate Arch, Arches National Park, 2010. "Directly in front of us was a huge, stone saucer as if a whirlpool had drilled down into the stone, and on the opposite side of the saucer was the arch. It was dizzying. I clung on to Dan as though I might fall, and there was no sound but the noise of swifts that nest there."

3. Photograph from the family archives, a family picnic, Llynfi valley, ca. 1935. "When we travel by rail, we can gaze at the wild green spaces that surround our town like a nest."

4. Photograph from the family archives, Maesteg, ca. 1900.

"How she feels it riding on the engine's thundering clatter, gliding through the silence of trees, and faraway on the mountain, the sheep run in fright without making a sound."

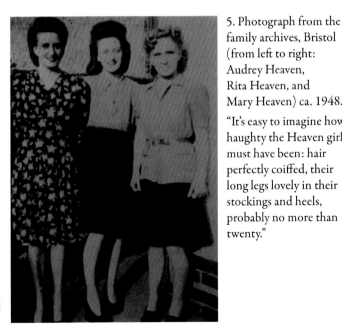

5. Photograph from the family archives, Bristol (from left to right: Audrey Heaven, Rita Heaven, and Mary Heaven) ca. 1948.

"It's easy to imagine how haughty the Heaven girls must have been: hair perfectly coiffed, their long legs lovely in their stockings and heels, probably no more than twenty."

6. Photograph from the family archives, Bristol (the marriage of Rita Heaven and James Brigley) ca. 1950.

"One day visiting at the nursing home, my grandmother says unexpectedly, 'All I ever wanted was a nice little house to call my own and take care of.' I believe her, but I am not sure that my grandfather did, at least at first."

7. Photograph by Zoë Brigley, *The Little Cage of Ellis Bell* exhibition, Hopkins Hall Gallery, Columbus: 1870-1875 White Cotton Corset and Poke Bonnet, 1840-49.

"Looking at the artifice of the hairpiece, the crinolines, and corsets on display, can we really say that the modern day is so different with our botox, padded bras, and Spanx?"

8. Photograph by Zoë Brigley, *The Little Cage of Ellis Bell* exhibition, Hopkins Hall Gallery, Columbus: Cage Crinoline, 1870-75.

"Our present moment has not progressed so much that we can gaze on these images without pause, because women's bodies are still caged by pressures, expectations, conformities."

9. Victoria Brookland, *Hawk*, ink and watercolor on paper, 2009.

"Brookland demands an escape from the stays and strings that bind. In *Hawk*, in the centre of a corset is a keyhole with one minutely written word: 'Fly'."

10. Victoria Brookland, *The Peregrine is Stronger*, ink, watercolor and collage on paper, 2013.

"Looking around the room, we see a hawk in the dress, a horse in the dress, an eye, a cathedral, a city in the dress, a ship in full sail, a building on fire. If the potential of women, their autonomy, and their desire, were finally released, the whole place might burn to the ground."

11. Photograph by Zoë Brigley, *The Little Cage of Ellis Bell* exhibition, Hopkins Hall Gallery, Columbus: dark brown silk satin damask gown with rose motif ca. 1840.

"The money to buy the brown dress may have directly or indirectly been a gain from the slave trade. Yet we might ask ourselves, how progressive is modern society when it comes to eradicating institutional racism, or xenophobia?"

12. Victoria Brookland, *The Little Cage of Ellis Bell*, ink and watercolor on paper, 2012.

"Victoria Brookland represents the possibility of being untethered to fly free, like the crow in *The Little Cage of Ellis Bell*, shown in the act of tearing an exit from the net of a crinoline with its beak."

III. Craft and Art

Good Bones

Over the summer of 2016, Maggie Smith's poem 'Good Bones' went viral. 'Life is short,' the poem begins, 'though I keep this from my children', and the preoccupation with risk continues, as the poem moves from the wild indiscretions of misspent youth to a mother now recognising a dangerous world:

> For every bird there is a stone thrown at a bird.
> For every loved child, a child broken, bagged

Birds are often the subject of poetry, posing as the poetic muse, or even divine messengers. Here, however, for each bird that exists in the liberating act of singing or flying, there is a bird injured, and the poem brings us back to the figure of the child. The comforting image of the 'loved child' flips to an image that violates all hope, beauty, and innocence. The side of truth that we don't care to scrutinise is the child dehumanised, treated like a doll, or a piece of disposable rubbish to be discarded without a second thought.

Knowing Smith to be a deeply compassionate writer, it was no surprise that people all over the world were touched by her poem, which seeks hope in the face of bleakness. That this particular poem went viral, however, also tells the power of poetry especially when dealing with the dark undercurrents of society that we find hard to face.

Because whether we like it or not, we live in a violent society. However civilised we like to imagine ourselves, violence is integral to our culture. In an obvious way, violence emerges in our rituals and sports, but it is also an unavoidable aspect of human life in events like childbirth or death. Beyond the obvious, even benign, violence that inhabits human space, there is also the violence that we try to ignore. There are the violences of rape culture on women and non-binary people (and some men), particularly black women, trans women, and other minorities for example Native communities in the US. There is domestic violence, which begins with psychological and verbal violations and ends in the kind of domestic murder that has become commonplace in the news. There are violences against those who come to represent what is different from a supposed 'norm': the immigrant in the xenophobic talk of Brexit or the white, nationalist alt-right; the supposedly inherently criminal black in American prison-industrial complex; or the trans or non-binary person who refutes gender binaries.

Most of these violences happen because of an act of violent refusal. The British or American 'native' refuses to recognise the human need of the immigrant. The American police officer refuses to recognise the humanity of the black driver at a traffic stop. The prison governor refuses necessary medication to the trans- woman in prison, thus rejecting her human right to self-determination and autonomy. The domestic abuser refuses to recognise the needs of their partner, using their lover only as a means to shore up their deep and unquenchable self-doubt. Such acts signal the closing down of true communication, and the impossibility of love or compassion for others.

It is debatable as to why such violence persists, and there is insufficient space to tackle that question here, but what is fair to say is that we live in a dysfunctional society. Yet Maggie Smith's poem hints at a hope to move beyond the frightening dysfunctions that have manifested themselves recently in terror attacks, fascist anti-immigrant rhetoric throughout Europe, or the sinister 'charisma' of Donald Trump in his US presidential bid.

Too often opposition to such violence is framed as emotional

60

and therefore unreliable. In *The Promise of Happiness,* Sara Ahmed writes about the feminist killjoy who, supposedly out of hysteria or malice, destroys the joy of others, which really means exposing the privileges that encourage racism, sexism, and homophobia. Black women fighting racism become 'angry black women'. Individuals challenging homophobia are associated with the 'unhappy queer stereotype'. Women or non-binary people trying to leave domestic violence are hysterical or unreliable. Trans people trying to speak up for their rights are framed as immature or unbalanced.

Such disenfranchisement is unacceptable, but poetry might be a powerful voice for such groups. A poem might be an outpouring of spontaneous feeling, but it is also feeling that is crafted, moulded, fitted to a form, and forced to speak in the most eloquent voice possible. This is clear in a poem like Vievee Francis's 'Taking It' where she displays the impact of men's violence against women in the community described. In the final few lines, Francis's narrator imagines a 'heavyweight' (her father? her peer at school?) punching her, and the man apologises for having 'to love you this way.' Francis's surprising conclusion reveals that the violence of men against women is not simply a malicious act, but a moment set into motion by complex circumstances, and propelled by profound anxiety that ironically coexists with love. The men themselves are complicated, seemingly sorry for their actions, but still culpable and unable to change their behaviour. Such violence is more than an individual act, Francis tells us, but is a result of societal dysfunction.

To such nightmares poetry might be an answer, because instead of refusing or rebuking, poetry speaks to everything that embraces and accepts others in spite of their differences. Poetry demands that you stand on the edge of understanding and embrace uncertainty.

Don't tell me that violence is inevitable, that it has always been so, and always will be, because I refuse to believe it. The problem is that human beings are born into uncertainty, yet human culture does its best to ignore this very fact, creating certainty in nationality, or in being a native, or in being a man, or in being white, or in being straight, or in being cisgender, or a combination of all these things. If poetry can encourage us to embrace uncertainty, to know that there are no rules, to make us that little bit braver, it might be revolutionary. We could make this place beautiful, as Maggie Smith tells us.

On Dream Language
and Not Confessing

In the autumn of 1921, a young man waited nervously in the waiting room of Dr. Sigmund Freud's Vienna office. On finally being admitted, the young man talked with the doctor about poetry, about the power of dream language, and its possibilities for humankind. The doctor's reaction was perplexed, and before long he brought the conversation to a close, dismissing the young man, and moving on to another waiting patient.

That young man was André Breton, poet and founding member of the French Surrealist movement. Breton, who was introduced to Freud's 1899 study *The Interpretation of Dreams* during his World War One service as a psychiatric aide, remained fascinated by the idea of dream-work, but he maintained a combative relationship with Freud. While Freud thought the language of dreams could be used as therapy, Breton saw a potential philosophical key to the human condition. Inspired by free association, Breton created automatic writing, a strategy designed not only to reach the unconscious mind, but also to refuse bourgeois rules about human life and behaviour. In dream language, Breton saw a remedy for human despair, and the use of techniques like automatic writing certainly allowed a fantastic escape from the mundane cruelties of everyday life.

Poetry is often invoked as a catalyst for metamorphoses from despair to hope, from desperation to redemption. In his essay, 'The State You Are Entering', David Wojahn traces a vein of poetry about depression, noting the 'tradition of mad British versifiers' from John Clare onwards, contrasting the British lineage with the American 'middle generation' – Sylvia Plath, John Berryman, Robert Lowell *et al* – who all 'suffered bouts of acute mental anguish resulting in extended hospitalization.' Forerunners of confessional poetry like Walt Whitman or Allen Ginsberg were self-mythologisers, but the Confessional movement of the 1960s was different to what had gone before. Michael Schmidt explains in *The Lives of the Poets* that Confessional Poetry was among the first to 'deliberately deal the pay-dirt on themselves.' While Schmidt admits that 'poets have always complained and settled scores and licked their wounds', they have 'not for the most part opened their wounds and probed them before their readers'.

Opening up has always been a struggle for me. I was extremely quiet as a child, painfully so as a teenager, and this meant that very often, I refused to speak to strangers at all. It changed when I went to university, where I learned that by dressing up as someone else, I could evade the crippling shyness. But I would still relapse at times. I remember working as a classroom assistant for an art teacher who I found very difficult and sexist, so I would just lapse into absolute silence. He compared me to Alice from Lewis Carroll's *Alice's Adventures in Wonderland*. Maybe this was just another way of dressing up? Did I take on the Alice role on purpose to help me manage having to work with a difficult man?

Growing up, I spent a lot of time watching other people, and I was lucky to have a family who just accepted my oddness. Sometimes being silent is read negatively. I remember having an argument with a university colleague years ago, when he suggested that quiet students in creative writing workshops were always sub-par. I took issue with this assumption, but so often we want writers to be extrovert, charismatic, and outgoing characters, which might work unfairly against people who cannot perform that way. I admit I have often wished that I could be more like those writers who seem open, unguarded, and powerful in their self-assurance.

But where is the space for the quiet voice? And what does it mean to confess anyway? 'Confess' is a nuanced word, originating in the French *confesser* and thus to the Latin *confiteri* or *confessus* with the synthesis of *con* (signifying completeness) and *fateri* 'to confess' from *fari* 'to speak'. Complete speech or complete honesty represent the origins of the confession. It conjures the booth of the Roman Catholic confessional in which one is cleansed of sin, or it recalls lurid tabloid stories in which the reader is a voyeur on the misdeeds or peculiarities (often sexual) of celebrities and stars.

Poetry as therapy for the writer is hardly a new idea. Discussing creative writing in American prisons, Lisa Rhodes describes how inmates 'wrote their poems as a vehicle to reclaim their lives and to find a rationale for their existence.' For such women, poetry was 'the catharsis to help them through their struggles, the door in which they can recreate their life.' To confess then can be to acknowledge wrongs, to own up and admit to the past, and to make known one's failings, often in the hope of some redemption. Confessing might be the act of revealing oneself with the hope of receiving grace and forgiveness in return.

Such an opening up, however, can be dangerous in other ways for the writer. Confessional poetry is still regarded in some critical circles with suspicion. Deryn Rees-Jones in *Consorting with Angels* suggests that such doubt stems from a view of emotion in poetry as a kind of failing, and she goes on to note that such weakness is associated with 'the awfulness of femininity'. A sexist attitude that associates emotion with the feminine seems to inflect the reception of confessional poetry, but that still leaves the writer in a tricky situation. Wojahn's questions about the problems of writing the suffering of self become even more pertinent: 'How do you write poetry at a time when even tying your shoes seems a Herculean labour? And how do you talk to someone about such a frightening predicament?'

What role does the reader play in all this? And why is confessional poetry still so popular in spite of critics' suspicions and derision? Might there be a kind of power in playing the priest?

The act of taking up a judgmental role can create a feeling of authority. There's voyeurism too, as the poet offers a lurid glimpse of an inner life behind the mask. But might there be something more redemptive about reading a confessional poem too: the possibility of mutual understanding and sympathy? Between the writer and reader, there might be a kind of interaction that admits the frailty and weakness of human beings and a shared sense of how vulnerable we are – each to the other.

Poetry, however, does not have to be straightforward confession, though outright confessing is sometimes a first route in for young or new writers. Speaking to my students, I emphasise that being honest does not necessarily mean having to confess, and this is where dream-work can be particularly useful to the poet who wants to write about difficult, personal material. Since the publication of *The Interpretation of Dreams*, human culture has been informed in its understanding of dreams by the notion of the unconscious, a region of the human mind that acts as a repository for repressed sexual and aggressive thoughts. Much of Freud's writing was devoted to uncovering how such repressions emerged in dreams, slips of tongue or jokes for example. Slips of the tongue reveal our hidden sexual or aggressive thoughts, so when George W. Bush was giving a presidential address to a group of teachers, instead of thanking them, he announced that he would 'like to spank all teachers'. Similarly thought-provoking is the humour of the Marx Brothers, which often reveals latent aggression. 'Don't look now,' says Groucho to a pompous ambassador in the 1933 film *Duck Soup*, 'but there's one man too many in this room and I think it's you'.

What the dream, the joke and the slip of the tongue all have in common is how they relate to thoughts and feelings that we repress in everyday life. Desires and fears reveal themselves in glimpses via dreams, jokes and slips of the tongue, and dream-work can be useful in finding new ways to deal with personal material in poetry beyond the obvious confession. The unconscious is supposed to be an unknowable force within us, and yet that we know it exists is a contradiction. Like poetry, the unconscious is slanted and slanting, knowable and yet able to surprise and confound. Hélène Cixous goes as far as to say in 'The Laugh of the Medusa' that writing 'poetry involves gaining strength through the unconscious [...] because the unconscious, that other limitless country, is the place where the repressed manages to survive'.

In *The Interpretation of Dreams*, Freud describes two types of dream-work: condensation and displacement. Condensation describes the phenomenon in a dream where people and places overlap, so to use a hypothetical example, a building in a dream may have the stairs and hallway of your childhood home, but the walls and frontage of your current workplace. Similarly, a figure in a dream may have the hair and clothes of one person and the glasses and beard of another. The parts of the composite may seem random and unimportant, but Freud emphasises that where two parts – places or people – are drawn together, the dream is usually signalling a commonality, an important parallel that the unconscious is working out through dreaming. Analysing his own dreams, Freud finds that a composite figure is made of two authoritarian men who both intimidate him.

The other type of dream-work is displacement, a phenomenon when 'one of the dream thoughts seems to have entered the dream-content, but then to an undue extent'. Freud gives the example of a patient who dreams of climbing up and down stairs; Freud diagnoses her dream-thought as related to desiring relations with someone of another class, so part of the dream thought remains (i.e. the movement up and down on the stairs/ in class) to an undue extent. A symbolic movement in class relations becomes a physical movement.

Displacement and condensation can be seen at work in the famous dream sequence of Alfred Hitchcock's 1945 thriller *Spellbound*. The dream sequence sets were designed by Surrealist artist Salvador Dali, and the dream itself is extremely Freudian. The film narrative is seen from the perspective of psychoanalyst Constance Peterson, who is trying to help a man accused of murder, but he is also suffering from amnesia. 'John Brown' tries to unravel his amnesia by telling his dream to Constance and the Freudian father figure, Dr. Alex Brulov. By the end of the film, it is discovered that all the answers to the murder mystery lie in the dream:

> I seemed to be in a gambling house, but there weren't any walls, just a lot of curtains with eyes painted on them. A man was walking around with a large pair of scissors cutting all the drapes in half. [...] I was sitting there playing cards with a man who had a beard. He said, 'That makes 21 – I win.' But when he turned up his cards, they were blank. Just then the proprietor came in and accused him of cheating. The proprietor yelled, 'This is my place, and if I catch you cheating again, I'll fix you.'

The win with 21 at cards is displacement of a place: the Twenty One Club, a place 'John Brown' visited with the murder victim, and where the murderer threatened his friend. Apart from the symbols that are explained in the film narrative, other images conjured by Dali linger to convey disturbing feelings. The eyes on the curtains might signal the feeling of being watched, but the cutting of the eyes with scissors not only recalls the shock value of the 1929 Surrealist film *Un Chien Andalou*, but also offers a classic Freudian image of castration. The blank cards are echoed on film by the proprietor's face being completely blank, signalling perhaps his lack of humanity, or even his amorality.

The second part of the dream reveals more examples of dream language through Dali-esque symbols, and hidden subtexts:

> Then I saw the man with the beard. He was leaning over the sloping roof of a high building. I yelled at him to watch out. Then he went over – slowly – with his feet in the air. And

then I saw the proprietor again. He was hiding behind a tall chimney, and he had a small wheel in his hand. I saw him drop the wheel on the roof. Then I was running and heard something beating over my head. It was a great pair of wings they were chasing me and almost caught up with me when I came to the bottom of the hill. That's all I remember. Then I woke up.

The turning motion of the wheel refers to the turning of a revolver, the murder weapon. The pair of wings is displacement for Angel Valley, the site of the murder, but the mountains are replaced in the dream by the sloping roof. By the end of the film, it emerges that the man sliding down the roof to his death represents not only the murder victim killed on a ski slope, but the brother of 'John Brown'. A guilt complex has emerged because 'John Brown' pushed his brother down a sloping wall where the boy was impaled on a set of railing. The act of sliding down and falling brings together the recent murder and the originary 'Cain and Abel' narrative. A suitably grisly Hitchcockian backstory is slowly revealed through the film through Dali's artistry and the Freudian screenplay by Angus McPhail and Ben Hecht.

The concepts of displacement and condensation play an important part in Freud's ideas about dream-work. Theorist Jacques Lacan, however, made a connection between dream-work and poetry. Lacan compares condensation with metaphor and displacement with metonymy, an intervention that is interesting for the poet.

For a long time, as a young writer, I found it hard to write about difficult and personal material, and I suffered from a kind of writerly shyness. Ask any shy person though, and they will tell you that they have had to develop strategies for dealing with shyness. I always remember the poet David Morley's story about how he overcame his anxiety about speaking in front of crowds by becoming a bingo caller: sometimes you have to face your fear head on.

Morley also taught me the importance of having a persona for teaching and public speaking that both is and is not your self, or at least, your private self – the shy part of you – that can remain hidden from view. I was not ready for confession, and what is a writer to do when they need to put down experiences in words, but at the same time cannot reveal their deepest intimacies in an obvious or exposing way? Reading about dreams, and dream-work though, I began to find an answer, because as the composer-actor Guy Forsyth explains in the 2001 film *Waking Life:* 'The trick is to combine your waking rational abilities with the infinite possibilities of your dreams. Because, if you can do that, you can do anything'.

A Song Like a Branch of Cherries

Everything that is written will potentially be read, so it is wise to take care when deciding to put pen to paper. This is something that my mother told me when I was a teenager, and she should know, since wherever I chose to hide my letters, she would find them, and of course, read them.

No one knew the risks of putting words on paper – or was more exhilarated by those risks – than the Welsh poet Alun Lewis. His letters are poems. His poems are cherished missives that not only speak to particular people from the poet's life, like his wife Gweno and his mistress Frieda, but also speak to us, the reader, with an intimate voice.

Lewis's life and death mean that the epistolary form has special significance in his biography and works. Joining the army in 1940, the letter was Lewis's lifeline to loved ones, yet he had always rejoiced in the letter, corresponding with a variety of writers from Robert Graves to Welsh novelist Lynette Roberts. It was Roberts who recognised Lewis as a charismatic writer of letters, telling him: 'I like your letters, Alun, but I should be frightened if you came too near. I might fall in love with you. I might be disillusioned.'

That Lewis admires the power of great letter writers is clear in his poem 'Sacco Writes to His Son'. Nicola Sacco was an Italian-born anarchist in 1920s Massachusetts, who was convicted for a robbery and condemned to death. Paraphrasing Sacco's last letter to his son before his execution, Lewis writes that happiness is only found in the 'sharing of the feast'. Writing poem-letters was a bold act of sharing and self-exposure that did indeed give Lewis joy.

Lewis's letters are works of art that seek to seduce the reader and conjure a particular version of the poet. During the war, Lewis complains in his letters about the job of censoring soldiers' messages to the family back home. He feels depressed at reading their banal love letters, and he notes 'how simple and innocent men can be, especially the ones who write clumsily.' He mocks the 'semi-heroic attitude' with which the men describe their training, before admitting that his own letters are full of bravado too. Lewis has nothing but disdain for the sentiment in the letters sent back home, but contemplating his own censored missives, he describes how his messages to his wife Gweno 'sing out in my heart like a branch of cherries and seven singing dwarfs, louder than all the trumpets, and it's the only true meaning in the sunshine and scene.'

Letter writing offers a chance for sincerity and honesty, and it provided some relief for Lewis in trying to work through the deep, abiding depression that expresses itself in poems like 'All Day it Has Rained':

> Tomorrow maybe love; but now it is the rain
> Possesses us entirely, the twilight and the rain.

Like some of the twentieth-century Confessional poets that came after Lewis, there is controversy over Lewis's death with John Pikoulis suggesting that the accident with a revolver that ended his life was actually suicide. Lewis is not exactly a confessional poet, however. His poems are more like conversations overheard or letters intercepted – perhaps with part of the contents redacted.

Lewis writes poem-letters to other writers; in 'To Edward Thomas', he explores Thomas's influence noting that 'like you I felt sensitive and somehow apart,' while 'To Rilke' confesses that Lewis 'hungered for the silence you acquired / And *envied* you.' Other epistolary poems by Lewis draw on the routines of soldiers writing back home. Some recall the accounts of place and culture that occur in Lewis's letters to Gweno. Particularly powerful is

'Home Thoughts from Abroad', which is addressed to the West and challenges the imperialist values that the British take abroad with their army:

We bear the dark inherited disease

Bred in the itching warmness of your hand

Without the self-probing detail of writers to come like Lowell or Plath, Lewis still managed to write with a stark and profound sincerity, and the act of reading his poems can sometimes feel like a violation of precarious speech between one person and another. It is no coincidence that in his correspondence with his wife Gweno and his mistress Frieda Ackroyd, poems were often sent alongside love letters as an extension of the sentiments expressed.

Most beautiful of all are Lewis's poems for Gweno, which often address her and make her the centre of each epistle. Lewis writes seductively in 'War Wedding v. The Marriage Bed', while poems like 'Goodbye' make the couple's parting tangible whilst leaving the lovers forever bidding adieu, as Keats would put it. The separated lovers are reunited in the imagination, so in 'In Hospital: Poona (I)', Lewis writes: 'I knew that you were furled, // Beloved, in the same dark watch as I.' 'Postscript: For Gweno' perfects the togetherness that the couple have in the space of the poem:

If I should go away, Beloved, do not say
'He has forgotten me.' For you abide,
A singing rib within my dreaming side

Throughout Lewis's *oeuvre*, this perfection of life in art, the reinstatement of a Biblical rib, is a recurring theme.

The letters and poems offer a sense of authenticity and truth, and Lewis writes in both forms with the knowledge that a letter might not just be read by the person addressed, but by a larger audience once it is out there in the world, so it can potentially be a text consumed by an individual and a mass of readers. Reading Lewis's letters and poems retrospectively with a sense of his biography, it is important to understand too that letters not only perform for a wider public, but they can deceive, dissemble, and disguise the truth. Writing to Gweno in 1944, Lewis tells her that her letter 'will survive me and it will survive you' presumably as a text for posterity, but he adds too that the letter is 'something that no one can ever know.'

When Lewis wrote to Gweno of 'love in its hard shell, like a tall fruit' during 1943 on active duty in India, he was in a state of anguish over his infidelity and conflicted feelings towards his wife and his lover Frieda Ackroyd. 'The Way Back', a poem written by Lewis to his mistress, represents the moment out of all Lewis's works when he is the closest to the tendencies of the Confessional movement. The rain returns in this poem, but here it is 'shafted' and works to 'Feminise the burning land.' Addressing Frieda, he tells her that she is 'Burning in the stubborn bone', while:

> Soldiers quickened by your breath
> Feel the sudden spur and rush
>
> Of the life they put away

Desire ignites the soldiers reminding them of the loves back home, so far away and distant from the painful indignities of war. The conclusion of the poem finds Lewis among 'iron beasts' again, and 'in the brilliance of this pain', his only longing is to rediscover that hunger of desire: a passion:

> To be squandered, to be hurled,
> To be joined to you again.

Once again, Lewis uses the epistolary form not merely to seduce or confess, but to make out of his difficult and passionate feelings something greater than himself. Lewis's epistolary poems are painfully sincere, and they ask us to compare our own intimacies with those of the poet. In the act of letter writing, so much more profound than the tweet, email, or text, Lewis makes the people and places of his short life come alive with a vivid and searing beauty.

The Little Cage of Ellis Bell

This is a transcription of the speech given at the reception of the poetry/art installation 'The Little Cage of Ellis Bell' at the Hopkins Hall Gallery arranged with the Ohio State Historic Textiles and Costumes Collection at the Ohio State University June 15th 2017.

The past is another country. They do things differently there. These words from L. P. Hartley's *The Go-between* are probably a cliché now, and the idea that the past is a faraway country is certainly challenged by Victoria Brookland's art. In Brookland's images the world of nineteenth-century women writers seems very close indeed. This exhibition features Victoria Brookland's paintings which reimagine or engage with Victorian womanhood, often featuring quotations from nineteenth-century women writers like Emily Dickinson, or the Brontë sisters. Alongside these paintings are nineteenth-century items from the Ohio State University Historic Textiles and Costumes Collection: nineteenth-century corsets, gloves, a bonnet, a crinoline, and the sumptuous brown silk dress.

Surrounded by these objects, Brookland's pictures hit you in the gut. Each image has a kind of enchantment and magic about it, and this enchantment is very much bound to what it says about women. Each portrait features a dress, which stands as a ghostly vision, because the dresses are almost never inhabited by people. Brookland signals immediately that her series is not a commentary on real women, but on ideas of what women should be, and often

Brookland demands an escape from the stays and strings that bind. In *Hawk*, in the centre of a corset is a keyhole with one minutely written word: 'Fly'.

It goes without saying that the modern era has progressed since the nineteenth century, but Victorian ideas especially towards women and their sexuality still dominate aspects of Western culture. The Western world tends to regard the past with a gaze that foregrounds modern civilisation and condemns the barbarism of the past, yet so many attitudes to women's bodies expressed today are reminiscent of Victorian ideas. Women's bodies are still viewed as objects. Women's bodies are supposedly easily victimised. Women's bodies are even at times viewed as duplicitous and untrustworthy. Women's bodies are too often defined by how they meet patriarchal expectations. Our present moment has not progressed so much that we can gaze on these images without pause, because women's bodies are still caged by pressures, expectations, conformities. Looking at the artifice of the hairpiece, the crinolines, and corsets on display, can we really say that the modern day is so different with our botox, padded bras, and Spanx? Just as bad as these obvious ways that women modify their bodies, however, there are the more insidious prescriptions invested in a view of women as passive, generous, giving, irrational, permeable, compromised.

But Brookland's paintings are not all doom and gloom, because what the dresses contain has the potential to be subversive and powerful. Looking around the room, we see a hawk in the dress, a horse in the dress, an eye, a cathedral, a city in the dress, a ship in full sail, a building on fire. If the potential of women, their autonomy, and their desire, were finally released, the whole place might burn to the ground.

The patriarchal legacy of the nineteenth century is not an innocent subject however, even for women, especially white women, because there is always the uncomfortable presence of imperialism and colonialism. I included Brookland's image *The*

Peregrine is Stronger in my collection *Conquest* because it spoke to me about power and domination. The dress has a city built upon it, and the spires and domes recall Western religious and political power, its wealth founded upon the exploitation of developing countries that were seen as barbaric. An eye looks out from a peephole, as if trapped within, but on the right the peregrine falcon wings its way out. The word peregrine originates in *peregrinus*, Latin for foreign, from *per ager*, meaning through the field. Brookland seems to say, yes, imperialism offers a kind of power, but the peregrine is stronger in its foreignness, its flight *through* the field, and away from the European, imperialist nation state.

Brookland is right to draw attention to the problematic aspects of the nineteenth century. Items like this brown silk dress borrowed from our Costume and Textiles Collection have a history bound up with imperialism. One cannot consider the history of silk without recalling imperialist trade and the Silk Road across Asia. The money to buy the brown dress may have directly or indirectly been a gain from the slave trade. There is complicity in such items that provokes uncomfortable thoughts. Yet we might ask ourselves, how progressive is modern society when it comes to eradicating institutional racism, or xenophobia? So many thoughts are triggered by a dress, a ghostly remnant of an unknown life.

The fact that Brookland's dresses are not inhabited by bodies also speaks to a more expansive view of what womanhood (or the femininity associated with women) might represent. It is still taboo in many parts of Western culture for a man or boy to wear a dress, despite the fact that toxic masculinity has deadly consequences. Edward Hyde, governor of New York at the beginning of the eighteenth century was well known for his cross-dressing, and when challenged for opening the New York Assembly in a hooped gown, he told the crowd that he was simply doing his utmost to represent Queen Ann: 'You are all very stupid people not to see the propriety of it all. In this place and occasion, I represent a woman, and in all respects I ought to represent her as faithfully as I can.' Hyde nimbly evades censure by framing himself as a representative of the queen, and her dress as a symbol of monarchic power, albeit a dubious colonial one. What is more subversive about what he says, however, is the thought that femininity (as it is traditionally framed) is not just attached to womanhood, but potentially a part of every human being, with the potential to be explored and celebrated.

Victoria Brookland's paintings of dresses represent the possibility of the symbolic dresses being untethered from traditional notions of gender and sexuality to fly free, like the crow in *The Little Cage of Ellis Bell*, shown in the act of tearing an exit from the net of a crinoline with its beak. Ellis Bell of course was the pseudonym of Emily Brontë when she first published her novel *Wuthering Heights*, a strategy that allowed her and her sisters to enter the narrow world of nineteenth-century British publishing. Brookland seems to approve of such moves through, across, and around gender and sexuality, and she reminds us that even now, there are lessons we can learn through reimagining and reassessing the nineteenth century. For we have the language now – both words and images – through which to express what freedom might look like.

Miriam the Prophetess, or Seeking Justice for Non-binary Folx

In memory of Eli/Miriam Roe

In his poem, 'Tintern Abbey', William Wordsworth suggests that memories of beauty have more than a 'trivial' influence on 'that best portion of a good man's life, / His little, nameless, unremembered, acts / Of kindness and of love.' My mother used to quote these lines to me when I was a child to remind me of the importance of small acts of service to others, and I couldn't help thinking with sadness of the poem when I heard that Eli/Miriam Roe had died.

I met the Roe family after first moving to the United States. Life in Pennsylvania was not without difficulty, since the day I arrived in the States, I found out I had miscarried my pregnancy. My husband Dan hadn't bought a car yet, so we caught the bus to the doctor's. In the dark room, in the white light from the ultrasound, I could see the appalled expression on the technician's face. It was the first time Dan was to see the baby. 'Don't look,' I said, but it was too late.

It took a long time to heal from the loss, but in the meantime, there were dinners at the Roe house. Evenings sat out in the garden, or around the kitchen table, talking about food and books, laughing with the Roe kids: Nathan, and Eli/Miriam. At Pennsylvania State University, John Roe was a mathematics professor who worked with my husband, originally from England, and his wife Liane is a research nutritionist. They told us about their courtship: how John had wooed Liane across country with a series of beautifully written letters. They both loved the national parks like Yosemite, and John was a keen climber. The Roe family always offered small acts of kindness, and without that help I don't know how we would have survived the terrible loss of our arrival.

It was only after we moved away from Pennsylvania that I heard that Eli/Miriam Roe had come out as a trans man named Eli, and before dying had embraced a gender-neutral, non-binary identity and was using both the names Eli and Miriam while learning to understand this. The family acknowledged both names and, after Eli/Miriam's death, often used Eli/Miriam in writing (as I have done here).

Eli/Miriam came out in 11th grade, and became an advocate for LGBT Christians. Eli/Miriam was bullied, and struggled with depression, but went on to be instrumental in setting up the Penn State network, 'Receiving with Thanksgiving,' offering a safe space for LGBTQA Christians to worship. On the organisation's website, Eli/Miriam talked about setting up this space because 'circumstances arose in my home church which brought the perceived "fight" between my LGBT identity and Christian identity very close to home.' It was heartbreaking when we heard that Eli/Miriam had died by suicide in 2016 at the age of twenty-two, after which support for LGBTQ advocacy in Christian settings was continued by John and Liane Roe.

The Roe family gave me so many small kindnesses, and the grief that Eli/Miriam's death brought to the family was hard to see. Before their death, Eli/Miriam published an intriguing poem in *RFD* magazine, reproduced here with the permission of Liane Roe. The poem uses the Biblical figure of Miriam to praise identities that are complex, mutable, and evade normative categories, using a subtle reinterpretation of the Biblical scripture. I want to provide a close reading of Eli/Miriam's poem 'Miriam', considering its relationship with Biblical passages Exodus 15 and Numbers 12, which feature Miriam in triumph and disgrace. Though often defined by her relationships with men (daughter of Amram, sister of Aaron and Moses), Miriam is a Biblical prophetess (Exodus 20-21). Indispensable in the exodus from Egypt, Miriam ensures Moses's adoption by the Pharaoh's family, and sings of victory when pursuing Egyptian charioteers are swallowed by the Red Sea. Later, she is punished for challenging Moses's patriarchal authority, struck down with leprosy and exiled to the desert.

There is a personal significance to Eli/Miriam's choice of Miriam of course. The exploration of the Biblical figure is also an exploration of non-binary identity. An important figure in Jewish and Biblical traditions, Miriam is described by Ursula Rapp in *Feminist Biblical Interpretation* as 'a person [...] between different spheres, a boundary walker or 'fence-sitter'', and this identity is heightened in the poem, where uncertainty and ambiguity challenge traditional readings of Biblical scripture. The poem works to create a non-binary space through imagery and formal techniques that emphasise the mutability of gendered identities beyond heteronormative definitions.

Miriam

In preparation for Passover Seder
a woman places a full cup
of water
for Miriam, sister of
Moses
beside the cup of Elijah's wine.
In her heart, they are still holy.

When her parents spoke of Miriam, prophetess
snow-white with sore for questioning God,
struck with leprosy for saying 'Has not the Lord also spoken to me?'
the woman tried not to wonder if her point
wasn't that she heard God calling clearly in the desert and felt
      the spring

82

bubbling up inside her.
She tries not to wonder if Miriam was eager, rather than
    blasphemous
as when the army of the pharaoh was drowned in the Red Sea

perhaps Miriam felt the oceans turning inside her and said
'Throw me the horse and the rider
and let God do his work.'

perhaps she understood, as only women can
what a terrible thing it is to mistake
a fountain of life
for a body.

Instead of a blessing for Elijah, the woman prays, Meribah
may you find peace in the desert, a cup of water to your people
emptying yourself for them over and over but never
running
dry

'Miriam' offers a subtle and intriguing narrative, which unravels
through the meticulous use of variable length in the poetic lines.
The clipped, short lines of the first stanza map the steps of a
Passover ritual, the Seder. The poem references how Miriam in
recent years has become a hero for Jewish women. The act of
placing a cup in honour of Miriam is a deliberate ritual, as women
sometimes put a humble offering alongside the more sumptuous
cup of wine for the revered prophet Elijah. The two cups alongside
each other recall the names, Eli and Miriam. The line breaks are
very significant, emphasising the water in the cup, and how the
Biblical Miriam cannot be signified by her name alone, but only
with the label 'sister of', while Moses has no such appellations. The
poem challenges confining people to categories defined by
heteronormative, and patriarchal ideals.

Water is significant throughout the poem, and it recalls Miriam's well-rock which accompanied the Israelites on their journey through the desert. In his 2010 essay 'Miriam Rediscovered' for *Jewish Bible Quarterly*, Moshe Reiss describes how Miriam transformed the arid landscape, making 'the desert bloom with green pastures and beautifully scented flowers.' The possibility of mutability is not only remarkable, but nourishing and enriching, and this is a key point of the poem 'Miriam'. The possibilities are most subversive however for inner space ('in her heart'), a heart space within identity where complex versions of the self – Elijah and Miriam – can coexist.

The lines of the second stanza grow longer as they unravel the particulars of Miriam's story. The linebreak after 'prophetess' undercuts her authority with the story from Numbers 12; after questioning Moses's marriage to a Cushite wife, Miriam (though not her brother Aaron) is punished by God with leprosy, her 'snow-white' body associated with soreness and suffering. Critical commentary records the fragmented nature of this Biblical passage, and how the narrative moves from a comment about Moses's wife to a cruel, unusual punishment like a non sequitur. In the poem, the woman hearing the story has doubts about the passage too, where Miriam is traditionally interpreted as jealous towards Moses, or even racist and xenophobic against the Cushite wife. The listening woman polices her own doubts:

the woman tried not to wonder if her point
wasn't that she heard God calling clearly in the desert and felt
    the spring
bubbling up inside her.
She tries not to wonder if Miriam was eager, rather than
    blasphemous

There is an intriguing uncertainty about the phrasing of these lines in their use of the negative. The phrase 'tries not to wonder' censors the content of what follows, while 'her point wasn't' denies certainty. The lines pose the possibility of Miriam having authority to reach the divine despite her punishments (in the desert), but also leaves the potential for something else less tangible and clear: the uncertainty of faith. This state of sitting with complexity and uncertainty is forbidden however; the third section – an emphatic single line – announces the importance of this thought. The suggestion that Miriam might not be blasphemous but 'eager', is itself blasphemous, as signalled by the way in which the protagonist polices herself ('tries not to wonder').

The poem turns now to a more positive Biblical story of Miriam from Exodus 15, when the Pharaoh's pursuing charioteers are swallowed by the sea, and Miriam sings a victory song inspiring the Israelites to rejoice: 'Sing to the Lord, for he is highly exalted. Both horse and driver he has hurled into the sea' (Exodus 15.20). Into this story, however, the poem inserts a note of doubt and uncertainty. Why does Miriam feel 'oceans turning inside her'? Is it a savouring of the water's power, or a sense of emotional turmoil and regret at the spilling of human life? This ambiguity is heightened by the rewording of Miriam's song; no longer is she simply commenting on God's power, but she commands to '[t]hrow me the horse and the rider.' Would throwing the riders to Miriam be an act of salvation and mercy? This reinterpretation certainly cuts across notions of Miriam as jealous, power-hungry, racist, or xenophobic.

Instead, Miriam is represented as having an intimate and secret knowledge of human vulnerability, and the comment 'as only women can' is perhaps turning back to the poet's non-binary identities as Eli and Miriam. What the Biblical Miriam understands is the fountain of life, a religious symbol for God, which often signifies purity (Jeremiah 2.13, Zechariah 13.1, Song of Solomon 4.12, Proverbs 10.11, Proverbs 25.26) and is associated with the policing of God's authority (Proverbs 13.14, Proverbs 14.27). Mortal human beings – represented by the body

– are not compatible with this symbolic purity, decided by patriarchal traditions, and perhaps signalling more retrograde interpretations of scriptures on sexuality and identity.

The poem rejects the sterile purity of the fountain, and calls instead on Miriam's well, and the waters of Meribah. In Numbers 20, Miriam dies, and Rapp emphasises that Miriam's death 'expresses the distance from God', because 'Miriam dies in the valley, as would be known from the location of Kadesh [Meribah], while [her brother] Aaron dies on a mountain, in fact on its summit, a place that in itself suggests a closeness to God.' Miriam is an exile again, still the leper, but Numbers tells how after her death the waters dry up, and the people turn against Moses. On striking the rock with his staff, the waters begin to flow, but there are consequences. Reiss wonders: 'Is there a connection between Moses and Aaron striking the rock – instead of speaking – and their consequent punishment of never entering the Promised Land and Miriam's death?' The poem imagines Miriam as the very waters of Meribah, or perhaps representing a force for ambiguity and complexity beyond supposed heteronormative certainty, and this is nourishing for all.

The poem ends with water ever-flowing, ever-changing, and ever finding a new path. The symbolism is both heroic and sacrificial, expressing admiration for a desire to nourish the lives of others, to give up something of oneself so that others might thrive. The poem seems to admire this self-abnegation, which recalls Eli/Miriam Roe's selflessness in advocacy work. John and Liane Roe described their child's selflessness even as a teenager in approaching the prejudice of others: 'Rather than yielding to anger or bitterness, Eli invested time and energy trying to build bridges between churches and the LGBTQ community.' Eli/Miriam's advocacy work is hugely admirable, yet 'Miriam' poses questions that illuminate considerations of Roe's life and work.

By the end of the poem, both the woman performing the Seder ceremony and Miriam have absorbed cruel patriarchal rebukes, the ignorance of their spiritual capabilities, and the incompatibility of their identities with the enforced sterility and supposed purity of the fountain. Not only must they absorb all of these injustices, but it is demanded that they continue to produce the waters that nourish others, just as Eli/Miriam continued to work for change in the face of prejudice and fear. Eli/Miriam often talked about the support and love received from family, but the surrounding institutions were not always so kind. It is too much to expect a well to never run dry in the face of hostility and cruel indifference, but the poem leaves us with such a predicament. Eli/Miriam deserved better. It behooves communities (including spiritual and religious ones) to provide support for individuals who face crushing forces of conformity, and it is this kind of justice and ally-ship that non-binary communities need and deserve.

New Worlds, New Imaginaries:
#metoo and #timesup

This is a transcription of a speech given at a United Nations campaign Heforshe event at the Ohio State University, March 3rd 2018.

I want to begin by quoting a short poem by the British author Jane Commane. The poem is called 'Landmarks' and it describes the threat of violence in our everyday spaces, questioning how or why we are supposed to negotiate that.

> Our geographies are different,
> Pierced by landmarks like this;
> Secluded lanes, alleyways, parks,
> emptying train carriages, taxi cabs,
> stairwells, public toilets, almost all
> open spaces when unaccompanied.
>
> Then, those other landscapes of threat;
> working late alone, short-cuts home,
> the party where the first drink swipes
> your running feet from under you,
> the stranger or the friend you trusted.
>
> It can happen almost anywhere.
> And too often, it does.
> We fold up this tattooed map of threats,
> carry it everywhere we go.

This poem was published a few years before #metoo went viral on social media, but it is certainly prescient in mapping out the prevalence and routineness of sexual and gender violence in everyday spaces: spaces where we work, public spaces that we have to negotiate in order to live our lives, intimate spaces that are supposed to be safe. In this assessment of how things have changed, I would like to consider #metoo and the journey that we have already started towards understanding this phenomenon, before considering possibilities for the future for #timesup and beyond.

I speak to you this evening as someone who has been working to correct perceptions of sexual violence for over ten years in my academic work, and in my teaching. Very often doing the work I do has felt like living in a parallel universe. In the world of my everyday life, sexual and gender violence is so often ignored, sidelined, covered up, while my research revealed the horrifying extent of the problem.

The prevalence of sexual and gender violence was also revealed to me through my work with students, and in fact some of the work that I am most proud of has been in helping students come to terms with experiences of violence through creative writing. On poetry courses that I have taught in the US and in England, one particular workshop is on dreams, and it puts forward the idea of using dream language – symbols and surreal stories – as a means to talk about the difficult or troubling moments from one's life. Sigmund Freud described dreams as enacting 'the liberation of the spirit from the pressure of external nature, a detachment of the soul from the fetters of matter', and for these students, writing about their lives as dreams gave them a sense of freedom, and allowed them to write about events even if they still felt ashamed or guilty about what happened. What became clear in holding these workshops is that many of the participating students wanted to write about sexual and gender violence (especially women and minorities), and it occurred with greater and greater regularity over the years. It was through my teaching then that I began to see how widespread such violence is. As an activist, an educator, a creative writer, and a survivor, I began to realise that I was not alone.

In fact, the classroom has the potential to be a life-changing, transformative space for all involved. It is worth remembering that the #metoo movement began in the 1990s in a classroom setting. Civil rights activist Tarana Burke was working in a school, when, as the *New York Times* reports, she was confronted by a thirteen-year-old girl who began to tell Burke about her experiences of sexual abuse. Burke was shocked by the admission, and she felt frustrated by her own inability to comfort this young girl. In an interview with Sandra Garcia for the *New York Times,* Burke describes how 'I didn't have a response or a way to help her in that moment [...] It really bothered me, and it sat in my spirit for a long time.' The answer that Burke invented was #metoo, because as Burke explains: 'We use a term called "empowerment through empathy." And "Me Too" is so powerful, because somebody had said it to me—right?—and it changed the trajectory of my healing process once I heard that.'

So this is where we have come so far, finding each other, finding empathy and a kind of collective voice, a kind of collective power. But that has also meant finding out hard facts about the way in which violence works. How though it falls on all of us who have said #metoo, it falls hardest upon the poor, on folx of colour, on those who do not fit conventional ideas about what gender or sexuality look like, non-binary people, and though men often perpetrate violence, they can also be victims of it too. We know now that it is not enough just to have empathy with white celebrities, but we must go forward by protecting the most vulnerable, and that means groups including but not limited to black women, immigrants, trans-people, bisexuals, non-binary folx, and Native American women. (I mention these groups in particular because they have been pinpointed as suffering particularly high rates of violence.)

And now we come to the question that is what all of us here tonight really care about: having found each other, what do we do about this violence? One initiative being set up is gathered around the hashtag #timesup. Set up in response to the momentum after the exposure of Harvey Weinstein's abuses, #timesup seeks to take practical measures to combat sexual harassment in particular, one notable aspect being a $13 million legal defence fund based in the National Women's Law Center, and the emphasis is on helping women on low-incomes who want redress for workplace harassment or assault. #timesup's defence fund seeks to help the most vulnerable people who may have even fewer resources than we do, even if we are all survivors.

The point is that if we are seeking to redress and correct these violences, justice can't just be for rich white people, and one thing that I would like to see come out of #timesup is a radical kind of deep imagining. What do we need to create a world where this kind of violence does not happen? We need to think about poverty, and how that makes specific groups of people vulnerable. We need to think about rape culture and the myths that it promotes, including racist ideas about non-white women and their sexuality. We need to look at how LGBTQ communities are still stigmatised in media cultural narratives, especially trans people. We need to critique our institutions – the police, medical care, government, and we need to consider radical new forms of community or restorative justice, because the current justice system is not working well for victims, especially not for people of colour. We need to think about reproductive rights, and who seeks to control women's bodies. We need to think about sex education, and the scripts that young people are taught.

Another important aspect of mobilising against sexual and gender violence is the development of different strategies to combat different kinds of violence. Sexual harassment in the workplace is different to intimate partner violence for example, and street harassment is different to date rape. We can argue that there is commonality, but it is worth considering that one task before us is to create specific strategies to combat specific kinds of violence.

And how might we enact the ideals of #timesup on campus and in the world? Campus has been proven to be an extremely dangerous public space. Documentaries like the 2015 feature *The Hunting Ground* have brought attention to what researchers in this area have known for a long time: that sexual and gender violence are pervasive on campus. Most studies tend to find that around 25% of female students have experienced sexual violence, a number that is probably suppressed due to under-reporting, as are the numbers for men and non-binary people who experience violence, where under-reporting happens due to specific, different kinds of stigma. So what can we do?

We can work on our institutions. Wherever we work or live, we need to examine what is being done by institutions to protect vulnerable subjects. Are schools providing proper sex education? Are there anti-violence advocates at local hospitals?

We can work at preventing violence. We need to ask ourselves how we can support or help to deliver educational programmes about consent or sexual scripts. We need to remember too that #timesup cannot just be a middle-class club. We can work with projects and charities in the wider community that are seeking to help poor and vulnerable subjects to find the resources they need.

We can consider the broader issues. This could mean everything from the erosion of LGBTQ rights, the demonisation of non-white people in the political sphere, or the denial of reproductive rights to women.

We can work with a mindset of change. Every day, I meet students who are budding social workers and lawyers, teachers and doctors, anti-violence advocates and counsellors, writers and dancers, and many take with them to whatever career they enter a readiness to challenge the way things are, and to make what change they can.

And finally, we can find joy in living. To be happy after experiencing violence is indeed subversive, because so often victims are labelled as irrevocably damaged. Of course, you cannot forget experiences of violence, nor should you have to, but whatever has happened in the past, we might have a chance to ensure that we can prevent violences from happening to future generations: we have a chance to make #metoo and #timesup so much more than hashtags. As Burke puts it in her interview, #metoo 'wasn't built to be a viral campaign or a hashtag that is here today and forgotten tomorrow, but was a catchphrase to be used from survivor to survivor to let folks know that they were not alone and that a movement for radical healing was happening and possible.'

Further Reading

I include this further reading list to share the things I have been reading and watching, which inspired these essays: the things that start the mind fizzing. The epigraph is taken from Gwyneth Lewis's collection, *Chaotic Angels* (Tarset, Bloodaxe, 2005) and is used with the permission of Neil Astley and Bloodaxe Books.

Arches

The description of Arches by Edward Abbey in *Desert Solitaire* (New York, Simon and Schuster, 1968 (1990)) is still wonderful, and Abbey has an incredible eye in describing the American landscape.

Frankenstein and Reproductive Rights

The essay that I mention by Claudia Dey, 'Mothers as Makers of Death', appears in *Paris Review* (August 14th 2018. https://www.theparisreview.org/blog/2018/08/14/mothers-as-makers-of-death/), and it seems to me to be a very important piece of writing about the way mothers are stereotyped versus the reality of motherhood. My writing here centres on Mary Wollstonecraft's *Frankenstein* of course, and my favourite edition is by Oxford University Press (1968 (1990), edited by M.K. Joseph). I also strongly recommend Fiona Sampson's biography, *In Search of Mary Shelley: The Girl Who Wrote Frankenstein* (New York, Pegasus Books, 2018).

Motherhood *is* Valuable for the Creative Life

The essay by Kim Brooks which I argue with in this essay is 'A Portrait of the Artist As a Young Mom' (*The Cut*, 2018. https://www.thecut.com/2016/04/portrait-motherhood-creativity-c-v-r.html). I also mention a beloved poetry collection

Gillian Clarke's *Letter from a Far Country* (Manchester, Carcanet, 1982).

Not *Breakfast at Tiffany's*

In this essay, I mention a number of key films including:

- *Breakfast at Tiffany's*. Directed by Blake Edwards, performances by Audrey Hepburn, George Peppard, Patricia Neal, Buddy Ebsen, and Martin Balsam, Paramount Pictures, 1961.
- *Fatal Attraction*. Directed by Adrian Lyne, performances by Michael Douglas, Glenn Close, and Anne Archer, Paramount Pictures, 1987.
- *Pulp Fiction*. Directed by Quentin Tarantino, performances by John Travolta, Samuel L. Jackson, Uma Thurman, Harvey Keitel, and Tim Roth, Miramax, 1994.
- *Single White Female*. Directed by Barbet Schroeder, performances by Bridget Fonda, Jennifer Jason Leigh, Steven Weber, and Peter Friedman, Columbia Pictures, 1992.

Also central to the essay of course is Truman Capote's novel *Breakfast at Tiffany's* (London: Penguin, 1958). I also highly recommend Gillian Flynn's novel *Gone Girl* (New York: Broadway Books, 2014).

Just a Woman with Nothing on Her Skin

If you want to read Laura Mulvey's full essay, 'Visual Pleasure and Narrative Cinema,' please see *Film Theory and Criticism: Introductory Readings*, edited by Leo Braudy and Marshall Cohen (New York, Oxford University Press, 1999, pp. 833-44). Also, one of the most intriguing and absorbing books I have ever read is the collected letters of Georgia O'Keeffe and Alfred Stieglitz in *My Faraway One: Selected Letters of Georgia O'Keeffe and Alfred Stieglitz: Volume 1, 1915-1933* (edited by Sarah Greenough, Ann Arbor CN, Yale University Press, 1968 (1990)). You can also find the report, 'USA: Stonewalled: Police Abuse and Misconduct Against Lesbian, Gay, Bisexual, and Transgender People in the U.S' on the Amnesty International website (2005. https://www.amnesty.org/en/documents/AMR51/122/2005/en/).

Turtle Hatching
The Beatles' song 'She's Leaving Home' appears on *Sgt. Pepper's Lonely Hearts Club Band* (Parlophone, 1967).

Life on Mars
David Bowie's song 'Life on Mars?' appears on the album *Hunky Dory* (Trident, 1971).

Fright House
This essay is inspired by Jean Baudrillard's *Simulations* (translated by Phil Beitchman, Paul Foss, and Paul Patton, Boston MA, MIT Press, 1983).

Nine Stories with Guns, and One Without
Larry McMurtry comes into this essay quite a bit. First there is his TV series *Lonesome Dove* (directed by Simon Wincer, performances by Robert Duvall, Tommy Lee Jones, Danny Glover, Diane Lane, and Angelica Huston, CBS, 1989), but I also quote McMurtry's essay 'American Tragedy' (*The New York Review*, January 11th 2011. https://www.nybooks.com/daily/2011/01/11/american-tragedy/). A few other key texts that come up are Sarah Kane's play *Blasted* (New York, Continuum, 2008) which I have taught for many years, the film *Carbine Williams* (directed by Richard Thorpe, performances by James Stewart, Conrad Salinger, and William C. Mellor, Metro-Goldwyn-Mayer, 1952), and the song 'Happiness is a Warm Gun', which appears on the Beatles' *The White Album* (Apple, 1968).

Good Bones
Maggie Smith's 'Good Bones' from *Good Bones*. Copyright ©

2017 by Maggie Smith. Reprinted with the permission of Tupelo Press, www.tupelopress.org. In this essay I also mention Vievee Francis's poem 'Taking It' which first appeared in *Muzzle* (https://www.muzzlemagazine.com/vievee-francis3.html). I also strongly recommend Sara Ahmed's study *The Promise of Happiness* (Durham NC, Duke University Press, 2010).

On Dream Language and Not Confessing

Sigmund Freud's *The Interpretation of Dreams* was at the heart of this essay, and I was using a particular edition: *The Interpretation of Dreams: The Complete and Definitive Text* (New York, Basic Books, 1899 (2010)). On poetry and depression, I find David Wojahn's essay illuminating: 'The State You Are Entering: Depression and Contemporary Poetry' (*New England Review* 17.1, 1995, pp. 110-123). Lisa Rhodes' essay, 'Poetry and a Prison Writing Program: A Mentor's Narrative Report', is also important, and you can find it in the *Journal of Poetry Therapy* (15.3, 2002, 163-168 (168)). I also mention a few other texts: Hélène Cixous's 'The Laugh of the Medusa' (trans. Keith Cohen and Pamela Cohen. *Signs* 14, 1976, pp. 875-893 (p. 879-880)), Deryn Rees-Jones's *Consorting with Angels: Essays on Modern Women Poets* (Tarset, Bloodaxe, 2005), and Michael Schmidt's *The Lives of the Poets* (New York, Vintage, 1998), which is a deeply enriching read.

A Song Like a Branch of Cherries

I was using a few Alun Lewis texts whilst writing this essay, including:

- *In the Green Tree: The Letters & Short Stories of Alun Lewis*, Swansea, Parthian, 2006.
- *Alun Lewis: Collected Poems*, edited by Cary Archard, Bridgend, Seren, 2009.
- Pikoulis, John. *Alun Lewis: A Life*, Bridgend, Seren/Poetry Wales, 1985.

Hannah Brooks-Motl's 'Learning the Epistolary Poem' is a

great introduction if you want to find out more about the epistolary poetry (*Poetry Foundation* website, 2013. https://www.poetryfoundation.org/articles/70050/learning-the-epistolary-poem).

The Little Cage of Ellis Bell

At the beginning of this essay, I quote L.P. Hartley's *The Go-Between* (New York, New York Review Classic, 1958 (2002)), and I also draw on Marc Schone's account of Edward Hyde in 'Power Cross-dressing' (*New York Magazine*, April 4 1994, p. 31).

Miriam the Prophetess, or Seeking Justice for Non-binary Folx

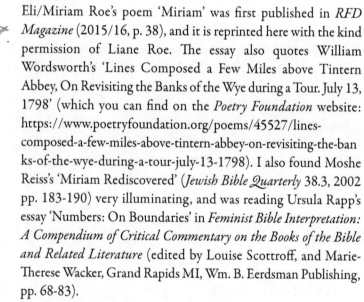

Eli/Miriam Roe's poem 'Miriam' was first published in *RFD Magazine* (2015/16, p. 38), and it is reprinted here with the kind permission of Liane Roe. The essay also quotes William Wordsworth's 'Lines Composed a Few Miles above Tintern Abbey, On Revisiting the Banks of the Wye during a Tour. July 13, 1798' (which you can find on the *Poetry Foundation* website: https://www.poetryfoundation.org/poems/45527/lines-composed-a-few-miles-above-tintern-abbey-on-revisiting-the-ban ks-of-the-wye-during-a-tour-july-13-1798). I also found Moshe Reiss's 'Miriam Rediscovered' (*Jewish Bible Quarterly* 38.3, 2002 pp. 183-190) very illuminating, and was reading Ursula Rapp's essay 'Numbers: On Boundaries' in *Feminist Bible Interpretation: A Compendium of Critical Commentary on the Books of the Bible and Related Literature* (edited by Louise Scottroff, and Marie-Therese Wacker, Grand Rapids MI, Wm. B. Eerdsman Publishing, pp. 68-83).

New Worlds, New Imaginaries: after #metoo and #timesup

This essay reprints Jane Commane's poem 'Landmarks', with the permission of the author, her editor Neil Astley and Bloodaxe

Books. The poem can be found in Jane Commane's collection, *Assembly Lines* (Tarset, Bloodaxe, 2018). To find out more about the originator of the #metoo movement, Tarana Burke, please see Sandra E. Garcia's interview 'The Woman Who Created #MeToo Long Before Hashtags' in *The New York Times* (October 20 2017: https://www.nytimes.com/2017/10/20/us/me-too-movement-tarana-burke.html). Finally, I mention a very important document film about sexual violence on campus: *The Hunting Grounds* (directed by Kirby Dick) which, ironically, was distributed by the Weinstein Company in 2015.

Images

1. Photograph by Zoë Brigley, Arches National Park, 2010.
2. Photograph by Zoë Brigley, the Delicate Arch, Arches National Park, 2010.
3. Photograph from the family archives, a family picnic, Llynfi valley, ca. 1935.
4. Photograph from the family archives, Maesteg, ca. 1900.
5. Photograph from the family archives, Bristol (from left to right: Audrey Heaven, Rita Heaven, and Mary Heaven) ca. 1948.
6. Photograph from the family archives, Bristol (the marriage of Rita Heaven and James Brigley) ca. 1950.
7. Photograph by Zoë Brigley, *The Little Cage of Ellis Bell* exhibition, Hopkins Hall Gallery, Columbus: 1870-1875 White Cotton Corset and Poke Bonnet, 1840-49.
8. Photograph by Zoë Brigley, *The Little Cage of Ellis Bell* exhibition, Hopkins Hall Gallery, Columbus: Cage Crinoline, 1870-75.
9. Victoria Brookland, *Hawk*, ink and watercolour on paper, 2009.
10. Victoria Brookland, *The Peregrine is Stronger*, ink, watercolour and collage on paper, 2013.
11. Photograph by Zoë Brigley, *The Little Cage of Ellis Bell* exhibition, Hopkins Hall Gallery, Columbus: dark brown silk satin damask gown with rose motif ca. 1840.
12. Victoria Brookland, *The Little Cage of Ellis Bell*, ink and watercolour on paper, 2012.

Acknowledgements and Thanks

Writing from this collection has appeared in: *The New Welsh Review, Planet: the Welsh Internationalist, Wales Arts Review, Poetry Wales, The Manifest-Station, Junction Box,* and *Agenda.* Essays here also appear in the anthologies *Far Villages: Essays for New and Beginning Poets* (ed. Abayomi Animashaun, Black Lawrence, 2019) and *Writing Motherhood* (ed. Carolyn Jess-Cooke, Seren 2017). Some of these essays were originally given as speeches: at a #timesup event for the United Nations Solidarity Campaign HeForShe (the Ohio State University, March 3rd 2018); at 'The Little Cage of Ellis Bell: Art/Poetry Exhibition' (Hopkins Hall Gallery, the Ohio State University, June 15th 2017); and as part of the Frankenreads Celebration at 'The Power of Frankenstein: A Kaleidoscopic Roundtable.' (the Ohio state University, 2nd November 2018).

Thank you to my colleagues at the Ohio State University for revealing the potential of prose: I was especially inspired by the spring when I observed Michelle Herman's workshop. Thanks to Liane Roe for allowing me to write about Eli/Miriam Roe's amazing poem 'Miriam'. Thanks to Emily Trahair, and Kathryn Gray for encouragement and support of my nonfiction writing. Thanks to the amazing anti-violence organisations that I have worked with in recent years including Heforshe, It's On Us, Advocates of Women of the World, and Proyecto Mariposas.

This book was completed as part of the research project 'Bodies in Transit 2: Difference and Indifference', funded by the Spanish Ministry of Education and Universities, Ref. FFI2017-84555-C2-2-P.